AF905035

Energy Law in Sweden

Energy Law in Sweden

Second Edition

Mikael Wärnsby
&
Madeleine Edqvist

This book was originally published as a monograph in the International Encyclopaedia of Laws/Energy Law.

General Editors: Roger Blanpain, Frank Hendrickx
Volume Editor: Kurt Deketelaere
Associate Volume Editor: Bram Delvaux

Wolters Kluwer

Published by:
Kluwer Law International B.V.
PO Box 316
2400 AH Alphen aan den Rijn
The Netherlands
Website: www.wklawbusiness.com

Sold and distributed in North, Central and South America by:
Wolters Kluwer Legal & Regulatory U.S.
7201 McKinney Circle
Frederick, MD 21704
United States of America
Email: customer.service@wolterskluwer.com

Sold and distributed in all other countries by:
Turpin Distribution Services Ltd.
Stratton Business Park
Pegasus Drive, Biggleswade
Bedfordshire SG18 8TQ
United Kingdom
Email: kluwerlaw@turpin-distribution.com

Printed on acid-free paper

ISBN 978-90-411-8549-5

e-Book: ISBN 978-90-411-8563-1
web-PDF: ISBN 978-90-411-8577-8

This title is available on www.kluwerlawonline.com

Printed and Bound by CPI Group (UK) Ltd, Croydon, CR0 4YY.

The Authors

Mikael Wärnsby was born on 9 October 1969 in Lund, Sweden, Mr Wärnsby graduated from Lund University in 1995 (LLM). After district court service, he was an associate and later specialist counsel in environmental law at Mannheimer Swartling Advokatbyrå (1997–2010), and adjunct judge of Hovrätten över Skåne och Blekinge (2010–2011). Since 2011, he is partner of Advokatfirman Lindahl. He is a member of the Swedish Bar Association (*advokat*) since 2000. His practice areas are environmental law and energy law, focusing on regulatory and contractual matters in the electricity, natural gas, nuclear power and renewable sectors.

Madeleine Edqvist was born on 13 May 1982. Mrs Edqvist graduated from Lund University in 2008 (LLM) and is an associate of Advokatfirman Lindahl, and a member of the Swedish Bar Association (*advokat*) since 2013. Her practice areas are mainly energy and environmental law with focus on regulatory and procedural matters.

The Authors

Table of Contents

List of Abbreviations

ARN *Allmänna reklamationsnämnden* (the National Board for Consumer Complaints)
bet. *betänkande* (Statement of Parliamentary Committees)
CCS Carbon Capture and Storage
CHP Combined Heat and Power (Facilities)
CO_2 Carbon Dioxide
dir. *kommittédirektiv* (Remits by the Government to Legislative Committees)
DSO Distribution System Operator
Ei *Energimarknadsinspektionen* (Swedish Energy Markets Inspectorate)
EIA Environmental Impact Assessment
EIFS *Energimarknadsinspektionens författningssamling* (the Official Gazette of the Swedish Energy Markets Inspectorate)
EUA EU Emission Allowance
EU ETS EU Emissions Trading Scheme
GHG Greenhouse Gases
GWh Gigawatt Hour or One Watt x 10^9 x Hour
KKVFS *Konkurrensverkets författningssamling* (the Official Gazette of the Swedish Competition Authority)
kWh Kilowatt Hour or One Watt x 10^3 x Hour
LNG Liquefied Natural Gas
MWh Megawatt Hour or One Watt x 10^6 x Hour
MÖD *Mark- och miljööverdomstolen* (the Land and Environmental Court of Appeal)
NAP National Allocation Plan
NJA *Nytt Juridiskt Arkiv* (Judgments by the Supreme Court)
NO_x Nitrogen Oxides
PFE *Program för energieffektivisering i energiintensiv industri*
Prop. Proposition (Government Bill)
rskr. *riksdagsskrivelse* (Parliamentary Publications)
RÅ *Regeringsrättens årsbok* (judgments and decisions by the Supreme Administrative Court)
SDR Special Drawing Rights
SEK Swedish krona
SFS *Svensk författningssamling* (the Official Gazette)
SO_2 Sulphur Dioxide
SOU *Statens offentliga utredningar* (Published Reports of Legislative Committees)
SSM *Statens strålsäkerhetsmyndighet* (the Swedish Radiation Safety Authority)
STEMFS *Statens energimyndighets författningssamling* (the Official Gazette of the Swedish Energy Agency)
SUS *Svensk utsläppsrättssystem* (the Swedish Emission-Allowance Registry)

SÖ *Sveriges internationella överenskommelser* (International Agreements Concluded by Sweden)
TFEU Treaty of the Functioning of the European Union
TPES Total Primary Energy Supply
TSO Transmission System Operator
TWh Terawatt Hour or One Watt x 10^{12} x Hour
VAT Value Added Tax

General Introduction

Chapter 1. General Background: Geography and Population

1. The Kingdom of Sweden is a small nation in a big country. Sweden has 9.5 million inhabitants within an area of 450,000 square kilometre, which by area makes it the third largest country in Western Europe.

2. The country extends 1,572 kilometres from *Treriksröset* (69.1° N) in the north to *Smygehuk* (55.2° N) in the south, whereas the longest main land distance from the east to west is 499 kilometres. The western border between Sweden and Norway follows the Scandinavian mountain range, with the highest peak 2,104 meters above sea level. Sweden also shares land boundary with Finland to the north-east. The rest of the Swedish landmass is surrounded by sea: the Skagerrak and the Cattegatt to the west, the Baltic Sea to the south and east, and the Gulf of Bothnia to the north-east. The country's largest rivers run through the province of Norrland and flow out in the Gulf of Bothnia.

3. Sweden's geography is characterized by its long coastlines, large forests and numerous lakes. More than half of the country's area is covered by forests. The forests are dominated by coniferous trees, in southern Sweden often blended with deciduous trees as birch, beech and oak. About 17% of the country's area consists of mountains and almost 9% of lakes and rivers. The cultivated land makes up only 8% of the land area.

4. Sweden's climate is shaped by the country's location in the border zone between Arctic and warmer air masses, as well as its proximity to the Atlantic. Considering its geographic location, which is one of the most northerly in Europe, Sweden enjoys a favourable climate, mainly due to the Gulf Stream which contributes to a milder climate than in many other places at the same latitudes. Over the period 1961–1990, the average temperature in January was 0°C in the most southern part of Sweden, while the coldest valleys in northern Sweden had an average temperature of -17°C. In July, the maximum average temperature was around +17°C in the south and just over -10°C in the north.[1] Average annual temperature over the period 1991–2007 was around one degree higher than in the period 1961–1990. The winter of 2007/08 was the warmest of all winters since the beginning of temperature measurements in 1858/59.[2]

1. www.smhi.se.
2. Ds 2009:63, pp. 6 and 17.

5. The country has approximately in average 5,000 population-weighted actual heating degree-days, second in European Union (EU) only to Finland, which has 5,500.[3]

6. Sweden's approximately 10 million inhabitants are unevenly distributed over the country. Approximately 80% live in cities or towns in the south of the country, whilst northern Sweden is sparsely populated. Approximately one-third of the population lives in the metropolitan areas of Stockholm, Göteborg (Gothenburg) and Malmö.

3. Eurostat, Heating degree-days by NUTS 2 regions – annual data, http://appsso.eurostat.ec.europa.eu/nui/show.do?dataset=nrg_esdgr_a&lang=en (Last update: 6 Mar. 2012). The average in the EU is 3,000.

Chapter 2. Basic Economic Characteristics

7. During the end of the nineteenth and beginning of the twentieth century, Sweden developed quickly from a poor agrarian country to one of the world's strongest industrial nations. The point of departure for this 'Swedish industrial miracle' was the country's natural wealth of forests, iron and hydroelectric power, as well as a long series of ingenious inventions.

8. Timber, hydropower, iron and other ores still constitute the resource base of an economy greatly dependent on foreign trade and exports. The main exports are machinery, manufactured goods, iron ore, steel, motor vehicles, chemicals and forest products. The main export destinations are other Nordic countries and countries in Western Europe, accounting for 64% of total exports (2014).[4]

9. The Swedish economy suffered a structure-crises in the mid 1970s and early 1980s, as well as deep recession in the first half of the 1990s. Thereafter, the economy recovered significantly with an average GDP growth (at market prices) of 2.8% per year until the financial crisis in 2008. In 2009, GDP declined by as much 5.0%, but recovered by 6.6% in 2010 and by 3.7% in 2011, which is significantly better than the Euro-area average. After a minor decline in 2012, the growth rate has been 1.2% in 2013 respectively 2.3% in 2014. Sweden is a member of the EU, but voted no to the common currency in a 2003 referendum. In 2014, GDP was Swedish Krona (SEK) 3,900 billion (app. Euro (EUR) 410 billion). The unemployment rate for August 2016 was 7.5%.[5]

4. Swedish Trade Agency: http://www.business-sweden.se/contentassets/4c591ba02d7b49e2877c3d5a2ffd92d7/sveriges-export-2014.pdf.
5. National Institute of Economic Research (*Konjunkturinstitutet*), www.konj.se and Statistics Sweden (*Statistiska Centralbyrån*), www.scb.se.

Chapter 3. Legal and Administrative Structure

§1. The Constitution

10. Sweden is a constitutional monarchy with a parliamentary form of government based on a one-chamber legislature. The King is the Swedish head of State (*statschef*), but since 1974, the function of the monarch is that of a representative and symbolic character only. Sweden is member of the EU since 1995.

11. The basic provisions defining how Sweden shall be governed, as well as the fundamental freedoms and rights of the Swedish people, are enshrined in the Constitution.

12. Sweden has four fundamental Acts which jointly form the Constitution: (1) the Instrument of Government (*Regeringsformen, SFS 1974:152*), which contains the most important provisions on the governing of the Kingdom, as well the main constitutional principles; (2) the Freedom of the Press Act (*Tryckfrihetsförordningen, SFS 1949:105*); regulating the freedom of speech and the right of access to public documents; (3), the Fundamental Law on Freedom of Expression (*Yttrandefrihetsgrundlagen, SFS 1991:1469*); and (4) the Act of Succession (*Successionsordningen, SFS 1810:926*), which regulates the heritage of the throne.

13. In addition to the Constitution, the supremacy of other legal frameworks has to be observed.

14. As a member of the EU, Sweden is bound by the EU's *acquis communautaire*, which *inter alia* means that legislation jointly enacted on an EU level in general take precedence over the national legislations of the Member States.

15. Further, according to the Instrument of Government, no legislation may be promulgated in conflict with Sweden's undertakings under *the European Convention for the Protection of Human Rights and Fundamental Freedoms* (*ECHR*), which has been transformed into Swedish law.

§2. Parliament

16. Sweden is a parliamentary democracy, which means that all public power emanates from the people. At the national level, the people are represented by Parliament (*Riksdag*) which has legislative power. Parliament is elected in general, direct and proportional (modified Saint-Laguë system) elections every four years. Parliament is unicameral and has 349 seats.

17. Under the Instrument of Government, the main functions of Parliament are to enact laws, determine national finances, supervise the Government and exercise control of the public administration. Another central task of Parliament is to determine national expenditure and revenue. The Parliament elects the Prime Minister (Head of Government), who appoints the other members of the Government (Ministers).

§3. The Government

18. The Government is organized in different departmental ministries (in 2016, ten), which all are led by a Minister appointed by the Prime Minister. The Government governs the nation and is the driving force in the process by which laws are adopted or changed, by way of submitting bills to Parliament. The Government implements the decisions made in Parliament. The Government is accountable to Parliament and must have the support of Parliament in order to carry through its policies.

19. In addition, the Government has certain legislative powers of its own. First, Parliament can, subject to limitations concerning various central fields of legislation, authorize the Government to issue ordinances in a number of areas. In Sweden, this kind of legislative technique is commonly used. An act, adopted by Parliament, often lays down the principal provisions for the legislation in question, whereas the Government, pursuant to the same act, is authorized to issue one or several ordinances containing detailed provisions supplementing the act.

20. Second, the Government may always issue, through ordinances: (i) rules concerning the enforcement of laws and (ii) rules, which are not – according to any of the Acts of the Constitution – supposed to be issued by Parliament. However, this 'residual competence' of the Government never excludes legislative competence of the Parliament in the same area (Instrument of Government, Chapter 8, section 7).

21. When the Government is allowed to legislate through ordinances, it may in general also delegate this task to subordinate authorities under its auspices (Instrument of Government, Chapter 8, section 11).

§4. Central Government Authorities

22. There are currently (2016) approximately 450 central government agencies (authorities), including commissions appointed by the Government to prepare coming legislation, accountable to the Government and for which the various ministries act as principal. The activities of the central agencies extend to Sweden in its entirety. Examples of such central agencies are the Swedish Energy Agency, the Swedish Energy Markets Inspectorate and the Swedish Environmental Protection Agency. In size as well as organizational respects, they differ considerably from each other, which is attributable to their varying functions. The primary function of these bodies is to implement the decisions taken by Parliament and the Government, e.g., by way of issuing administrative regulations, recommendations and advice in their different operation areas, but also to supervise subordinate local organs (usually municipalities) as well as individual operators with respect to the conformance to various regulatory legislation.

23. All government authorities, including the county administrative boards (*see infra*), are autonomous, in the sense that they operate on their own responsibility, but in accordance with guidelines drawn up by the Government. The system of ministerial rule, often found in other countries, does not apply in Sweden.

§5. Regional Governance

24. Sweden is divided into twenty-one counties (*län*). Political tasks at this level are undertaken on the one hand by the county councils (*landsting*), whose decision-makers are directly elected by the people of the county and, on the other hand, by the county administrative boards (*länsstyrelser*) which are government authorities in the counties.

25. The tasks of the county administrative boards are, apart from promoting and monitoring the development of the county, *inter alia* to be responsible for state administration in the county to the extent no other authority has been specially designated for this purpose. This also encompasses the exercise of supervision in various fields, and also often the function of determining appeals in individual cases.

§6. Local Governance

26. Sweden has 290 municipalities (*kommuner*). Each municipality has an elected assembly, the municipal council, which takes decisions on municipal matters. The municipal council appoints the municipal executive board, which leads and coordinates municipality work.

§7. The Judicial System

I. Main Principles

27. The independence of the Swedish courts is safeguarded by the Instrument of Government according to which neither the Government or any authorities, nor the Parliament may determine how a court should adjudicate in a particular case (Chapter 11, section 3).

28. The Instrument of Government contains a general rule on judicial review (Chapter 11, section 14), pursuant to which a court can set aside a provision which conflicts with the Constitution or another provision of a superior statute. Traditionally, Swedish courts have been cautious in exercising their right of judicial review, although, under the influence of EU law, this institute gradually tends to be more frequently used.

29. Furthermore, the Council of Legislation (*Lagrådet*), which is composed of judges of the Supreme Court (*Högsta domstolen*) and the Supreme Administrative Court (*Högsta förvaltningsdomstolen*), checks important legislative proposals in relation to, among other things, their constitutionality. The opinions of the Council of Legislation normally have great importance, although they are not binding on the Government or Parliament.

II. Organization of the Court System

30. Like several Continental European countries – but in contrast to its Nordic neighbours Denmark and Norway – Sweden's court system is divided in two parallel branches – the *general courts* and the *general administrative courts*.

31. In addition, there are a number of *special courts* whose jurisdiction is restricted to disputes relating to certain parts of the substantive law, such as land use and environmental law (the land and environmental courts), labour law (the Labour Court) and certain aspects of competition law (the Market Court).

III. General Courts

32. In simplified terms, the general courts adjudicate cases which have not been expressly excluded from their jurisdiction. This includes the majority of civil law cases as well as (all) criminal cases. The system of general courts consists of three instances: district courts (*tingsrätter*, being the courts of first instance), courts of appeal (*hovrätter*, six such courts) and the Supreme Court (*Högsta domstolen*). Leave of appeal (*prövningstillstånd*) has to be granted in order for a case to be tried by the Supreme Court, and there is a strict screening process of cases to this end.

IV. The General Administrative Courts

33. The general administrative courts mainly adjudicate appeals against decisions of the administrative authorities (unless otherwise provided by law).

34. The general administrative courts play an important role in the regulatory energy law area, since they, as the main rule, handle appeals against decisions of the regulatory authorities under, *inter alia*, the Electricity Act and the Natural Gas Act.

35. The system of general administrative courts also consists of three instances: general administrative courts of first instance (*förvaltningsrätter*), the administrative courts of appeal (*kammarrätter*, four such courts), and the Supreme Administrative Court (*Högsta förvaltningsdomstolen*). Like the Supreme Court, leave of appeal to try cases before the Supreme Administrative Court is granted under special circumstances only.

V. Special Courts

36. As mentioned *supra*, the special courts deal with cases in specific areas of substantive law.

37. Of particular interest for the energy law area are the land and environmental courts and the Market Court.

38. The land and environmental courts handle cases regarding certain environmental permit and concession matters, building permits, urban planning, real property matters like right of way, etc. as well as cases regarding water operations and actions for injunctions and damages under the Environmental Code (*see infra*). Five district courts have the task to act as environmental courts. Appeals are made to the Land and Environmental Court of Appeal (*Mark- och miljööverdomstolen*, which constitutes a part of Svea Court of Appeal), as the middle instance, and from there to the Supreme Court.

39. The Market Court has jurisdiction in disputes concerning, *inter alia*, restraints in competition, marketing practices and contract terms in consumer relations.

Chapter 4. Energy Balance and Energy Policy

§1. Introduction

40. Swedish legislation in the energy law domain is to a notable extent influenced by the energy resources which are actually exploited, generated and consumed in the country, as well as by the energy policies that govern and guide these activities. For the understanding of Swedish energy law, this presentation starts with an overview of the consumption and supply patterns which constitute the Swedish energy balance and a summary of Sweden's energy policy.

§2. Energy Balance

I. Basic Production and Supply Characteristics

41. Since the mid-1980s, the supply to the Swedish energy system (Sweden's Total Primary Energy Supply (TPES)) has remained at a level between 550 and 600 TWH. In 2014, the amount of energy supply in Sweden TPES was 553 TWh. In 2014, nuclear fuel accounted for one-third of the energy. The level of nuclear fuel supply has been relatively constant since the mid-1980s. Oil (crude oil and petroleum products) accounted for 24%, 134 TWH, of the energy supply, while other fossil fuels (natural gas, coal and coke) amounted to 7%. Renewable energy sources (windpower, biofuel and hydropower) accounted for 37%.[6]

42. The country's electricity power generation is based mainly on hydropower and nuclear power. In 2015, the total electrical energy generated was 158 TWh, whereof and nuclear power accounted for approximately seven respectively 34% each. In the same year, the production of wind power set up a new record with 16.6 TWh (10% of the electricity production).[7] Electricity production from wind power has increased significantly in recent years.

43. In paragraphs 44–50 *infra*, we provide a more detailed description of the Swedish energy balance.

---

6. Statistics from the Swedish Energy Agency, http://www.energimyndigheten.se/statistik/energibalans/. Statistical treatment of nuclear and hydropower gives the impression that nuclear power generates significantly more energy than hydro power. In reality, this is not the case. The reason is that for nuclear there is efficiency losses in converting thermal energy from the nuclear, whereas hydropower has no such losses when converting water energy into electricity.
7. The Swedish Energy Agency, *The Electricity Year 2015*.

II. Total Energy Use

44. Energy is supplied to meet users' demand for energy. When describing the Swedish energy balance,[8] it is therefore relevant, as a point of departure, to provide certain statistics relating to the country's total energy use and how these figures have changed over the last thirty years.

45. In 2014, Sweden's total final energy use was 368 TWh, which is a further reduction compared with recent years. The energy use had the following allocation between different final user sectors and other categories:

- industry (39%);
- transport (23%);
- residential purposes and service sector (38%).

46. The same year losses, own use in the energy sectors and uses for non-energy purposes, were totally 186 TWh, of which conversion losses in nuclear power represented almost 63%.

47. Other losses constitute of distribution losses in the delivery of electricity, losses in heating and combined heat and power stations and use for non-energy purposes, such as raw materials for the chemical industry, lubricating oils and oil products used in the building and construction sectors, e.g., asphalt and surface coatings.

Conversion losses occur in connection with electricity and heat production, as well as in refineries and coking plants (*koksverk*).[9] Distribution losses occur in connection with supplies of electricity, natural gas and other energy gases, as well as in connection with district heating.

48. The industry and the residential and service sectors use (in aggregate) essentially the same amount of energy now as in 1970, although the underlying consumption basis has changed significantly over the years. For example, the number of houses and buildings to be heated has increased, population numbers have risen by about 18%, and industrial production has increased considerably in comparison to 1970. Further, a gradual changeover from use of oil to electricity has caused conversion losses to be 'moved' to the supply side of the energy system.

49. The major increase of energy use has occurred in the transport sector (excluding international maritime traffic). In comparison to 1970, the energy use in this sector has increased by 60% in 2014.

50. The use of energy varies between the years. Annual differences in temperatures and weather influence the use of energy in the residential and service sectors, whilst variations with respect to the industrial sector are mainly due to economic factors, such as growth and the state of the market.

51. The total use of electricity, including losses in transmission, was 136 TWh during 2015, which together with 2014 have been the lowest level during the twenty-

---

8. The description of the Swedish energy balance in paras 44–51 is based on statistics from the Swedish Energy Agency (http://www.energimyndigheten.se/statistik/energibalans/) and *Energy in Sweden 2015*.

9. In the statistics, 'conversion losses' also include the energy sector's own internal use. Conversion losses in hydropower production are not included in statistics.

first century, which is explained by warm climate in Sweden. High production rate and low electricity use lead to a large amount of electricity export from Sweden to neighbouring countries; 2015 was a record year as Sweden's net export of electricity reached 22.6 TWh.

III. Total Energy Supply

52. In 2014, the total energy supply in Sweden was 553 TWh. Since 1970, the total energy supply has increased by 25%. It is notable that during the same period (1970–2014), the demand for energy has decreased by 2%. As mentioned under paragraphs 44–50 *supra*, electricity has to a large extent replaced oil in the two user sectors industry and residential and service. The supply of crude oil and oil products has fallen by over 45%, while the supply of electricity has increased by over 240% – mainly as a result of the expansion of nuclear and hydropower production.

53. From the users' point of view, electricity is a highly efficient energy carrier, but significant conversion losses occur in the production stage. Consequently, the changeover from oil to electricity has caused much of the conversion losses to be transferred from the end users to the supply side of the energy system (*see also supra*).

54. In the 1980s, district heating systems were expanded by several local (municipal) energy utilities, and pipeline transmitted natural gas was introduced in the southern and western parts of the country. Supplies of coal and coke for fuel purposes increased in the beginning of the 1980s, but have been declining since then. In the mid-1990s, favourable subsidies from the Government resulted in a start of construction of larger wind power plants, both onshore and offshore.

55. In 2015, out of the total domestic electricity production of 158 TWh, hydropower produced 74 TWh (47%), while nuclear power accounted for 54 TWh (34%). Hydropower production varies widely during the year, depending on the amount of precipitation. In the same year, fuel-based thermal power production (including industry) produced 13.5 TWh of electricity (8.5%), while wind power contributed with 16.6 TWh (10%). The wind power production increased with almost 45% compared to the previous year 2014. In international terms, Swedish energy use includes a relatively large proportion of energy from renewable sources, including bio fuels, hydropower and wind power. In 2015, approximately 52% of the country's total energy use originated from these sources.

§3. Energy Policy

I. The 1997 and 2002 Energy Policy Decisions

56. Over the years, Swedish energy policy has to a large extent been characterized by a political consensus among the large parties of the Parliament with one major exception: nuclear power. In 1997, the Social Democrats, the Centre Party and the Left Party Agreed on an energy policy later manifested in the government bill (prop.

1996/97:84) which was approved by Parliament the same year. The main goals of the 1997 energy policy was *inter alia* to secure the supply of energy under competitive conditions in an international perspective, to establish the prerequisites for an efficient energy use and cost-efficient energy supply, gradually phasing-out nuclear power and facilitate the transition to a sustainable society with a minimum of negative effects on the environment. In 2002, Parliament adopted a government bill (prop. 2001/02:143) for an updated energy policy. Under the 2002 energy policy, the main objectives set out in the 1997 policy decision remained, however, with certain changes and amendments. In 2002, Parliament also adopted a climate strategy, containing climate targets for 2010 and 2050.[10]

57. Changes in the 2002 energy policy concerned primarily the support mechanisms intended to encourage the development of renewable energy sources. It was envisaged that direct state aid should be abolished under a transition period and replaced by more market-orientated support mechanisms.

58. Trade in electricity certificates (green certificates) was introduced in 2003 (*see* further *infra*), in order to encourage the production of energy from renewable sources. The electricity certificate system also aims at supporting different sources of renewable electricity in a competitively neutral manner.

59. As regards the phasing-out of nuclear power, the 2002 energy policy decision envisaged that representatives of the energy sector and the industry should negotiate with the Government in order to reach an agreement on a long-term phasing-out of nuclear power production, which, however, has not resulted in an agreement.

II. The 2009 Climate and Energy Policy

60. Following the 2006 election, a centre-right coalition (presently in 2013 in power) formed the Government. This resulted in a change of the energy policy, primarily with respect to Swedish nuclear power for which the earlier phasing-out policy was abandoned. However, many other fundamental elements of earlier policies were confirmed, including the goals of further reduction of carbon dioxide (CO_2) emissions and the ambition to avoid direct subsidies for renewable energy sources, except the support offered by the electricity certificates system.

61. Thus, in 2009, Parliament approved a new climate and energy policy according to the government bills 'An Integrated Climate and Energy Policy'.[11] The basis for the climate and energy strategy is *inter alia* the EU energy and climate policies and the common goal to achieve a limit in the rise in temperature to no more than 2 degrees Celsius above the pre-industrial level. The 2009 climate and energy policy is also founded on the climate policies of the EU and the so-called 20-20-20 target.

62. The purpose of the policy is to provide a foundation for the future efforts that need to be made in order to contribute to a stabilization of the greenhouse gas concentration at a level that enable the climate targets adopted by the EU to be reached. According to the 2009 policy, Sweden's climate and energy targets for 2020 are (i) 40% reduction in greenhouse gas emissions compared to the 1990 level, (ii) at least

10. Prop. 2001/02:55.
11. Prop. 2008/09:162 and Prop. 2008/09:163.

50% renewable energy, (iii) 20% more efficient energy use, and (iv) at least 10% renewable energy in the transport sector. The long-term vision for 2050 is that Sweden will have no net emissions of Greenhouse Gases (GHG) into the atmosphere. The target of a 40% reduction in greenhouse gas emissions relates to the non-trading sector, i.e., sectors not included in the EU Emissions Trading Scheme. It therefore relates *inter alia* to transport, housing, waste facilities and parts of industry.[12]

63. As regards the renewable target, the electricity certificate system is to be developed. The goal for the production of renewable energy is an increase by 25 TWh in 2020 compared to 2002. The national target for wind power energy is an annual production capacity of 30 TWh in 2020, whereof 20 TWh onshore and 10 TWh offshore.

64. For vehicles, the policy sets out a long-term target according to which vehicles in Sweden shall be independent of fossil fuels by 2030 and also an overall target of a 20% reduction in energy intensity between the years 2008 and 2020.

65. Other important objectives of the 2009 policy are, as mentioned *supra*, the abolishment of the decision to phase-out nuclear power, the development of a common Nordic end-customer market for electricity and the increased interconnection of the electricity networks in other countries.

66. The ways of reaching the above targets (as described *infra*) include new legislation, government proposals to modify taxes and implement more stringent economic policy instruments. EU legislation and policies, as well as international agreements and commitments, are of significant importance towards achieving these targets.

12. Prop. 2008/09:162, p. 12.

Chapter 5. Historical Background and the Development of Energy Law

67. Sweden's rich hydropower resources contributed to the country's rapid industrialization by the end of the nineteenth and by the beginning of the twentieth century. This relatively cheap energy source enabled the exploitation of Sweden's other important natural resources as ore and forests, and to the establishment of several large-scale and energy-intensive industries (such as steel, pulp and paper). Notably, the Swedish traditional industry sector is still proportionally larger than those of its Nordic neighbours and most other European countries of a comparable size.

68. At the same time, Sweden is characterized by its considerable geographical distances and a relatively cold climate, which makes transmission of electricity a crucial issue *inter alia* since most hydropower resources are located in the north, whilst large parts of the energy-consuming industry and the vast majority of the population are found in Central and South Sweden.

69. Given this background, it is logical that the origin of large parts of Swedish energy law – which is still very much traceable today – can be found in the legislation concerning electricity, water and minerals.

70. The first Swedish Electricity Act was enacted in 1902, and remained in force – although subject to reforms over the years – even up to 1997, when the present Electricity Act came into force in connection with the deregulation of the electricity market, which was achieved a year earlier, in 1996. At the time of the adoption of the previous Electricity Act in 1902, two of the major concerns were to protect the public from personal damage and damage to property, and to legally enable the construction of high-voltage power lines on land owned by third parties. The main principles of the old electricity regime – which was characteristic by regional or local monopolies both with respect to networks operations and electricity supply (by a few vertically integrated energy companies) – remained in force until the deregulation of the electricity market commenced in the 1990s. This issue is dealt with separately under Part I regarding electricity, *infra*.

71. Water rights, for example concerning rights to build mills, were codified as far back as in the medieval law-rolls of the Swedish provinces. The first modern Water Act came into force in 1919. Many of the principles laid down in the Water Act of 1919 – although changed and supplemented over the years and subject to a major reform in the 1980s when the new Water Act of 1983 was enacted (now incorporated in the Environmental Code) – are still valid. This concerns *inter alia* the fundamental question of rights to water and water resources and the basic scope of application of the water legislation.

72. Also, the Swedish mining legislation has very old roots. Since the seventeenth century, it has been based on a mining-claim system whereby the person who first discovered a mineral resource in principle was entitled to obtain the sole right to explore and exploit the deposit following the fulfilment of certain formalities. This mining-claim system has been the basis of subsequent twentieth century Mining Acts of 1938 and 1974, and is still a fundamental principle in the current Mining Act, which entered into force in 1992. The need of the state to control mineral exploitations in Sweden in conjunction with the industrialization, led to the successive introduction of a concession system – a system that ultimately originates from principles proclaimed during the French Revolution and which apply in different forms in several countries in the world – for the exploitation of different kinds of minerals from the nineteenth century and onwards, which system under the current Minerals Act covers nearly all commercially exploitable minerals.

73. In order to meet increasing energy consumption demands during the second half of the twentieth century, Sweden developed a significant nuclear power capacity, in which the first reactors were taken in commercial operation in the beginning of the 1970s. In addition, pipeline transmitted natural gas was introduced in Sweden in the beginning of the 1980s, which was later than in most countries in Western Europe.

74. The introduction of these new energy sources prompted the introduction of specific legislation concerning nuclear activities (the Atomic Energy Act of 1956, replaced by the 1984 Nuclear Activities Act), nuclear liability (the Nuclear Liability Act of 1968 that will be replaced by Act on Liability and Compensation due to Radiological Accidents of 2010 upon sufficient international ratification), radiation (the Radiation Protection Act of 1988), as well natural gas (the Pipelines Act of 1978 and the Natural Gas Acts of 2000 and 2005).

75. During the 1960s, growing awareness and concerns regarding the environmental situation – internationally as well as in Sweden – led to the introduction of legislation particularly aiming at protecting the environment. In Sweden, the Nature Conservancy Act came into force in 1964. It was followed by several additional environmental statutes; *inter alia* the important Environmental Protection Act in 1969. In particular, the latter Act gave the State extended means of controlling and monitoring environmental hazardous activities, and it obliges operators to limit emissions of harmful substances and to clean up and remediate polluted areas. With effect from 1999, a large number the previous environmental statutes, including the 1983 Water Act, were amalgamated into the Environmental Code, which is an attempt to create increased uniformity in the environmental law domain. In later years and in particular since Sweden became a full member of the EU in 1995, the development of EU environmental law has had significant impacts on Swedish environmental law. One important current issue on the EU level, especially in the energy area, is the introduction of so-called flexible mechanisms, such as emissions trading, in order to reduce greenhouse gas emissions. The interaction between energy law and environmental law is further dealt with in Part IV, *infra*.

76. In addition to the development of environmental protection rules, the deregulations of various – previously more or less monopolistic – markets have been in focus during the last decade. This development is also largely driven at the EU level, and has led to the introduction of several important concepts – *inter alia* Third-Party Access (TPA) to networks and unbundling of networks operations from supply business – which characterize both the electricity and the natural gas sectors. Also, the regulatory frameworks for the prices charged by the natural monopolies (transmission and distribution networks) in these sectors gradually tend to become more detailed and complex, in particular in comparison to the situation of the early years of deregulation in the 1990s. Moreover, market deregulation is closely connected to competition law, and the Swedish Competition Act is modelled on EU competition law.

77. Since the beginning of the 1990s, energy taxation has been actively used as a tool to reach certain energy policy goals, such as reduced green house gas emissions. In connection with the tax reform of 1990, Sweden began a process which has been denoted a 'green tax shift'. The intention of this process is to increase energy taxes and impose certain emission taxes (such as the CO_2 tax, the sulphur tax and the levy on nitrogen oxides ($NO_{x)}$ which were introduced in 1991–1992), while other taxes (such as income tax) were decreased by equivalent amounts.

78. Another tool that has been used to support preferred energy production sources (i.e., renewables) is direct subsidies. However, direct subsidies currently play a limited role in Swedish energy system, in which market-based support mechanisms are favoured. Such mechanisms include the electricity certificates system, which was introduced by virtue of the Electricity Certificates Act in 2003, and the emissions trading scheme, which was launched in the EU in 2005 (EU ETS). The electricity certificates system has recently been enlarged to cover a common Swedish-Norwegian market. Also, the EU ETS is subject to a successive development under different 'trading periods' (the third starting 2012), aiming at gradually reducing the number of emission allowances on the market and the inclusion of additional sectors and GHG in the trading system.

Chapter 6. Basic Principles of Energy Law

§1. Energy Law as a Legal Discipline

79. From a Swedish perspective, energy law does not, at present, constitute a legal domain with distinct boundary lines vis-à-vis other legal domains. In general, energy law is not treated as an 'independent' legal discipline. From a systematic point of view, Swedish scholars often tend to deal with energy matters as a special branch of environmental law. However, the concept of 'energy law' can be described from several different legal perspectives, depending on which questions that are in focus.

80. Nevertheless, it seems fair to say that Swedish law in the energy field (like environmental law), as a whole, falls under the domain of administrative law. This is true both with respect to main regulatory legislation on electricity, natural gas and nuclear power, as well as with respect to the rules in the Environmental Code and other environmental legislation on, *inter alia*, exploitation of natural resources (such as water for hydropower and minerals), construction and operation of different energy generating facilities, and emissions trading.

81. In all those areas, public authorities pursue several important tasks and, in general, permit procedures and other legal proceedings have an administrative law character. Here, it could be noted that even though Swedish environmental courts are civil law courts, the procedure in matters (in particular regarding permit matters) handled by them show many elements of an administrative law character, e.g., with respect to the investigations that have to be performed before decisions are taken and regarding publication requirements at different stages of the proceedings.

82. Further, several aspects of the use of real property, e.g., planning and development of land and water, as well as property formation (including the formation of public easements and utility easements) are generally subject to administrative law provisions and proceedings. In addition, the competition law aspects of energy law – which have been in focus over the last decade largely due to deregulations of energy markets – contain several elements of administrative law. Also, the tax law aspects of energy law fall under this legal domain.

83. In a wider sense, however, energy law touches upon civil law too. This is the case as to *inter alia* general real property issues (ownership, rights of user, etc.), compensation matters in connection with damage and disturbance from energy operations on real property and matters on certain precautionary measures. Evidently, commercial trade in electricity, natural gas, oil, etc. mainly falls under the domain of contract law.

84. In this presentation, we will deal with energy law mainly from the administrative law point of view referred to above. Thus, focus will be put on the regulatory parts of the legislation. However, specific matters regarding *inter alia* trade and damage and liability, as well as certain private law issues in the competition law domain will also be addressed.

§2. Certain Main Concepts of Swedish Energy Law

85. The structure of the legislation, which regulates energy law matters is, as already indicated and as in many other countries, complex. Swedish energy law is not systematically governed by one comprehensive act or codification – partly in contrast to, for example environmental law (an area closely connected to energy law), where the Swedish legislator recently has strived to compile the majority (but far from all) of the most important environmental statutes into one single act (the Environmental Code of 1998), which regulates not only substantial environmental issues but also procedural, administrative, criminal and certain civil law matters of environmental law.

86. Instead, energy law matters are regulated by a plethora of different statutes which aim to handle different aspects of, e.g., generation, transmission and consumption of the 'goods' (such as electricity, natural gas or oil), whereas other legislation primarily deal with environmental, safety and market issues. Predictably, the regulatory framework also varies significantly due to the special features of the energy sector in question.

87. However, despite this rather complex legal structure, the following general principles may be distinguished:

(1) *Natural resources* used to produce energy (e.g., waterfalls) belong to the landowner where the resource in question is located, but may be claimed and used by third parties if such use lies in the 'public interest', subject to (in general) different kinds of compensation to the landowner concerned.
(2) *Exploitation* of minerals and other natural resources for energy generating purposes (such as uranium, natural gas, oil, coal or peat), generally requires different forms of concessions (licences) and/or environmental permits.
(3) *Generation/operation* of heat or electricity from different sources (e.g., hydropower facilities, thermal power plants, wind power plants, etc.) is subject to various environmental permit requirements and conditions.
(4) *Network operations*– i.e., the construction and operation of power lines and pipelines – with respect to the networks for electricity, natural gas, oil and district heating are subject to special concession requirements.
(5) *Network access* by third parties (TPA) is a precondition for the functioning of a deregulated market where customers can freely choose their supplier. In Sweden, a complete TPA regime is in place in the electricity sector where the market is fully deregulated, as well as in the natural gas market.
(6) *Connection tariffs and network tariffs* for access to the electricity and natural gas networks are subject to price control based on *inter alia* EU legislation. In Sweden, price control of electricity tariffs is from 1 January 2012 performed *ex ante*, meaning that tariffs are approved by the regulatory authority in advance. An *ex ante* regime similar to the electricity tariff system is proposed to be introduced for natural gas.
(7) *Trade in and marketing of* electricity, natural gas, district heating and other energy forms or means of producing energy are not subject to any concession, licence or permit requirements. Furthermore, there is no regulation on prices regarding

the 'energy carrier' (product) as such (electricity, natural gas, etc.) – hence, the principle of freedom of contract applies.

(8) *Incentives* to support the favoured energy policy goals are frequently used. Such guide measures include *inter alia* taxation on different fuels and emissions and market-orientated mechanisms, such as trading in electricity certificates and CO_2 emission allowances.

(9) *Framework legislation* is a technique commonly used by the Swedish legislator in the energy sector (as well as in many other fields of administrative law). This means that general provisions or principles are laid down in acts enacted by Parliament, whilst the Government or authorities under the Government, often are given rather far-reaching authorizations to supplement the provisions of the acts in question with more detailed provisions in ordinances or regulations.

Chapter 7. Role of Government Institutions in the Shaping of Administration of Energy Law and Policy

§1. The Setting of Energy Policies

88. Parliament sets the governing policy for the energy sector based on bills submitted by the Government. At the time of writing, the Ministry of Enterprise, Energy and Communications (*Näringsdepartementet*) has the overall coordination and planning role for the Swedish energy policy.

89. When formulating the policy, the Government has to take into consideration the legislation and policies of the EU and, among other issues, the legal framework for the creation of internal markets for electricity and natural gas, as well as the implementation of flexible mechanism to reduce greenhouse gas emissions, such as emissions trading.

90. The authorities under the Government have the task to implement policies and other decisions on the basis of guidelines of the Government and in accordance with the relevant legislation.[13] An overview of the main authorities under the auspices of the Government in the energy sector will be given *infra*. For the comprehension of their role to implement energy policies and administrate energy law, certain important characteristics of the Swedish administrative system in general shall however first be addressed.

§2. Characteristics of the Administrative System

91. The central government agencies (authorities) are responsible for implementing decisions made by Parliament and the Government. The mandate of each central authority is laid down in a separate ordinance issued by the Government, such ordinances containing specific instructions and guidelines for the work of the authority in question (*myndighetsinstruktioner*). The central authorities are frequently given the mandate to issue administrative regulations (*föreskrifter*), which are binding, based on authorizations from the Government in ordinances. Such regulations contain detailed provisions for a specific area, as supplements to the relevant act and ordinance. In addition, the authorities frequently issue general advice – which are non-binding – but may have significant impact as to the interpretation of different areas of administrative law. In addition, the central authorities often handle different applications for permits, approvals or subsidies (grants) submitted by natural or legal persons.

92. An important principle with respect to the role of Swedish public authorities is that their independence in decision-making is guaranteed by the Constitution. Neither

---

13. Pursuant to the Act on Municipal Energy Planning (*Lagen om kommunal energiplanering, SFS 1977:439*), the municipalities also fulfil certain tasks with respect to the coordination of energy planning measures within the geographical area of the municipality.

the Parliament nor the Government may determine how an administrative authority shall make its decision in a particular case concerning the exercise of public power in relation to a private party or a municipality (Instrument of Government, Chapter 12, section 2). Thus as mentioned, the principle of ministerial rule, often found in other countries, does not apply in Sweden.

93. Naturally, this does not mean that authorities have a full discretion in decision-making. They have to act in accordance with law and within their competence as decided by the Government. Decisions of authorities which have factual or legal effects for another party can, as the general rule, be appealed to a general administrative court or, in certain cases to superior authorities and/or ultimately to the Government. The Government's decisions can in certain cases – in accordance with the principles laid down in Article 6 of the European Convention on the Protection of Human Rights (ECHR) – be made subject of legal review by the Supreme Administrative Court pursuant a special Act on Legal Review of Certain Administrative Decisions (*Lag om rättsprövning av vissa regeringsbeslut, SFS 2006:304*).

94. Moreover, the Swedish concept of supervision (*tillsynsmakten*) should be observed. The central authorities exercise supervision of the subordinate local organs (usually municipalities) and of persons or entities with respect to conformance of regulatory legislation. The supervisory function often involves powers to intervene when errors are discovered or suspected, e.g., by way of requesting information and/or to issue injunctions or fines. Supervisory functions in different areas – e.g., environmental law – are also often exercised by regional county administrative boards or municipal authorities.

§3. Principal Authorities in the Energy Law Domain

I. Swedish Energy Markets Inspectorate

95. The principal authority in the energy sector is the Swedish Energy Markets Inspectorate (*Energimarknadsinspektionen, Ei*). The Ei combines the roles of regulator, licensing authority and supervising authority for the electricity, natural gas and district heating markets. By delegation, it has the assignment to implement the decisions made by Parliament and the Government in the energy law area. The Ei supervises network operators in the electricity sector as well as in the natural gas area in accordance with the Electricity Act, the Natural Gas Act and the District Heating Act. Moreover, the Ei handles concession applications regarding construction and operation of electricity power lines and natural gas pipelines, assesses and approves revenue caps and certifies Transmission System Operators (TSO) for the electricity and natural gas markets.

II. Swedish Energy Agency

96. The Swedish Energy Agency (*Energimyndigheten*) is a government agency for national energy policy issues. The Agency's strategic work is *inter alia* to promote sustainable development in the energy sector, support the achievement of the national climate targets, ensure a secured energy supply and promote the enhancement of renewable energy sources. The Agency is also responsible for the managing of the register for the emissions trading system and the operation of the electricity certificates system.

III. Svenska Kraftnät

97. *Svenska Kraftnät* is a state utility (*affärsverk*), which administers and operates the national electrical grid. It also has system responsibility for balancing the Swedish electricity system. Further, Svenska Kraftnät is the authority responsible for Sweden's contingency planning with respect to power supply.

IV. Swedish National Electrical Safety Board

98. The Swedish National Electrical Safety Board (*Elsäkerhetsverket*) handles and supervises technical safety issues in the electricity sector in accordance with the Electricity Act.

V. Swedish Environmental Protection Agency

99. The Swedish Environmental Protection Agency (*Naturvårdverket*) is the central environmental authority under the Government. The Agency's main tasks are to implement environmental policy decisions on government grants and the application of environmental law, propose targets, measures and control instruments for environmental policy and environmental protection activities, as well as follow-up and assess the environmental situation and environmental efforts. In the field of supervision, the role of the Environmental Protection Agency is generally restricted to providing guidelines to regional and local authorities (county administrative boards and municipalities), that conduct the supervision under the Environmental Code. However, the Environmental Protection Agency has the general supervisory responsibility under the Act on CO_2 emissions and grants emissions allowances under the said Act.

VI. Swedish Radiation Safety Authority

100. The Swedish Radiation Safety Authority (*Strålsäkerhetsmyndigheten*) is the principal central authority under the Government with respect to nuclear activities. The authority is the regulatory authority under the Nuclear Activities Act. In this capacity, it supervises nuclear power plants and other nuclear activities in the country.

VII. Board of the Nuclear Waste Fund

101. The Board of the Swedish Nuclear Waste Fund (*Styrelsen för Kärnavfallsfonden*) administers the Nuclear Waste Fund, in accordance with the Act on the Financial Measures for the Management of Waste from Nuclear Activities (*SFS 2006:647*).

VIII. Mining Inspectorate of Sweden

102. The Mining Inspectorate of Sweden (*Bergsstaten*), which was established as far back as in 1637, is the agency responsible for the administration of mineral resources in Sweden. It reports to its controlling authority, the Geological Survey of Sweden (*Sveriges Geologiska Undersökning – SGU*). The main tasks of the Mining Inspectorate (under the Minerals Act acting generally through its director, the Mining Inspector) are to issue concessions under the Minerals Act for the exploration and exploitation of mineral deposits and, in its capacity as supervisory authority, to ensure compliance with the Act.

IX. Swedish Competition Authority

103. The Swedish Competition Authority (*Konkurrensverket*) has the general task to safeguard and increase competition in Sweden, *inter alia* in the energy sector (which is handled by its Department 3). It conducts supervision under the Competition Act. In addition to applying the Competition Act, the Authority provides proposals for changes to rules and other measures to eliminate obstacles to effective competition, as well as develops and disseminates information on competition issues.

X. Certain Other Authorities Handling Energy-Related Matters

104. Additional government authorities dealing with energy include:

- The Swedish Financial Supervisory Authority (*Finansinspektionen*) grants licences under the Securities Trading Act – which are required for certain trade in electricity certificates and emission allowances – and supervises trade in securities.
- The Legal, Financial and Administrative Services Agency (*Kammarkollegiet*) represents the State generally in matters concerning operations in public waters.
- The Swedish Civil Contingency Agency (*Myndigheten för samhällsskydd och beredskap*) is the supervisory authority under certain security-related legislation, *inter alia* the Combustibles and Explosives Act (*SFS 2010:1011*) and the Act on Measures to Prevent and Limit the Consequences of Serious Chemical Incidents (*SFS 1999:381*, the 'Seveso legislation').
- The National Board of Housing, Building and Planning (*Boverket*) is, among other tasks, responsible for promoting effective use of energy in buildings and the reduction of use of electricity for residential heating.

Chapter 8. Sources of Energy Law

§1. The Hierarchy of Norms

105. Sweden is commonly considered to belong to the Continental law tradition, which is characterized by its emphasis on statutory law.

106. From a general point of view, the sources of Swedish energy law are the same as for Swedish law in general: laws and other statutes, court precedents, preparatory works (*travaux préparatoires*), customs and commercial practice in the field of private law, and finally legal doctrine. Some brief remarks on certain parts of this general hierarchy of norms are given *infra*.

§2. EU Law

107. As a member of the EU, Sweden is bound by the *EU acquis communautaire*. In case of a conflict between a Community norm and a national norm, the Community norm shall prevail.

108. Energy is a sector where shared competence between the Union and the Member States applies according to Article 4 of the Treaty on the Functioning of the European Union (TFEU). The TFEU provides for several provisions for energy measures, such as Articles 170–172 TFEU, which provide for creation of trans-European networks, *inter alia* with respect to energy infrastructure. Article 194 TFEU states that the union policy on energy *inter alia* shall aim to ensure the functioning of the energy market, security of energy supply in the Union and promote the interconnection of energy networks.

109. EU has adopted a large number regulations and directives in the energy area, as well as different Council resolutions on a consistent energy law and policy within EU.[14]

§3. Acts and Other Statutes

110. *Constitutional acts* (*grundlagar*) and *ordinary acts* (*lagar*) are legal statutes enacted by Parliament. Enactment of constitutional law is performed by two identical decisions of Parliament where a general election takes place between the two decisions. An ordinary act requires one single decision by Parliament only.

111. *Ordinances* (*förordningar*) are norms that are enacted by the Government.

112. *Regulations* (*myndighetsföreskrifter*) are norms which are issued by central government authorities or regional or local authorities.

113. Constitutional acts, ordinary acts and ordinances are published in the Official Gazette, *Svensk författningssamling* (*SFS*). Regulations are published in

14. Cf. Krämer, *EC Environmental Law* 380 et seq. (Sweet & Maxwell 2011).

gazettes for each individual authority, such as the gazette published by the Swedish Energy Agency, *Statens energimyndighets författningssamling* (*STEMFS*).

114. The Official Gazette (SFS) is accessible *inter alia* via Parliament's database on the Internet at www.riksdagen.se. The gazettes of different authorities are in general published on the Internet home page of each authority (*see* Selected Bibliography, for further information on relevant Internet addresses).

§4. International Treaties

115. International treaties to which Sweden is bound are as such not part of Swedish law. In order to become part of the Swedish hierarchy of norms, they have to be transformed into Swedish national law. Transformation of a treaty follows a two-step procedure. First, a treaty concluded by the Government has to be approved by Parliament. Second, the treaty (or the substantive content of the treaty) has to be transformed into Swedish law by an Act of Parliament.

116. International treaties and agreements concluded by Sweden are published in the series *Sveriges internationella överenskommelser* (*SÖ*).

117. Examples of international treaties – to which Sweden is a party – of significance in the field of energy law are the Paris and Brussels Conventions on nuclear liability,[15] the Kyoto Protocol under the United Nations Framework Convention[16] and the Energy Charter Treaty.[17]

§5. Court Precedents

118. In Sweden, the judgments or decisions of the higher courts are not formally binding on the lower courts. Thus, the so-called *stare decisis* doctrine is not applicable. However, principles laid down by the Swedish Supreme Court and the Supreme Administrative Court are in practice closely adhered to by the lower courts. Further, judgments by lower courts (generally appeal courts) are in some instances used as guidance in other cases if no relevant precedent from either of the Supreme Courts exists.

119. The decisions of the Supreme Court are reported in Part I of *Nytt Juridiskt Arkiv* (*NJA*), and decisions by the Supreme Administrative Court in *Regeringsrättens årsbok* (*RÅ*).

15. *See* paras 197–203 *infra* .
16. *See* paras 626–630 *infra* .
17. The Energy Charter Treaty (signed in Lisbon on 17 Dec. 1994), is a legally binding, multilateral instrument, which focus on the protection and promotion of foreign energy investments, free trade in energy products, freedom of energy transit through pipelines and grids, reduction of environmental impact of the energy cycle through improving energy efficiency, and mechanisms for resolution of state-to-state or investor-to-state disputes.

§6. Preparatory Works

120. The preparatory works to Swedish legislation are not considered to be a formally binding source of law, but they have traditionally been regarded as important sources for the interpretation of an enacted law – unlike, for example, the preparatory works to EU legislation.

121. The most important preparatory works to Swedish legislation are found in the Government Bills submitted to Parliament (*proposition*). Guidance can also be sought in other documents made in the legislative process, e.g., the opinion by the Legislation Council, and – at an earlier step in the process – in the usually comprehensive reports (*betänkande*) of legislative committees appointed by the Government in order to inquire a certain matter under the terms of reference provided by the Government.

122. Almost all preparatory works to more recent Swedish legislation are accessible on the website of the Parliament at www.riksdagen.se.

123. The reports of the legislative committees are published in the printed series *Statens Offentliga Utredningar* (*SOU*). The more recent of these reports are available from the Government's website at www.regeringen.se.

§7. Legal Doctrine

124. The legal doctrine is not considered a source of Swedish law in the formal sense. Nevertheless, as in most other countries, certain texts by authoritative legal scholars have gained significant influence and have in practice come very close to a formal source of law.

Part I. Regulatory Framework Concerning Electricity

Chapter 1. Introduction

125. In this Part I, the main parts of the legal framework pertaining to production, transmission, trade and consumption of electricity, respectively are described.

126. In order to facilitate for the reader to place the different provisions in their relevant context, Chapter 2 provides a general overview of the most important parts of the legal framework that will be further addressed in the following chapters.

127. With respect to electricity production (*see* Chapter 3 *infra*), the focus will be on the two dominating electricity production sources in country: hydropower and nuclear power. Considering the explicit goals of the Swedish energy policy, a part of this chapter is also devoted to certain recently introduced mechanisms that aim at promoting electricity generation from renewable energy sources.

128. The legal framework concerning transmission, trade and consumption of electricity will be described in Chapters 4, 5 and 6, and respectively. Finally, Chapter 7 contains an overview of the institutional framework in the electricity sector.

Chapter 2. Legal Framework for the Electricity Sector: General Overview

§1. The Electricity Act

129. The fundamental provisions and basic principles of the Swedish electricity legislation are now consolidated in the Electricity Act (*Ellagen, SFS 1997:857*), which came into force on 1 January 1998.

130. The Electricity Act replaced both the old Electricity Act of 1902 (*Lag innefattande vissa bestämmelser om elektriska anläggningar, SFS 1902:71 s. 1*)[18] and the Electricity Trading Act (*Elhandelslag, SFS 1994:618*), which contained certain special provisions following the deregulation of the electricity market in 1996 (cf. Directive 96/92/EC).

131. One of the main objectives of the Electricity Act is to create a clear separation between the transmission of electricity (i.e., network operations), on the one hand, and activities concerning production of, or trade in, electricity, on the other. Trade in electricity (as well as generation or production) takes place on a free market subject to competition between several different players, and is not subject to any direct regulation under the Electricity Act or other instruments of legislation. Network operations on the other hand, constituting national, regional or local monopolies, fall under the provisions of the Electricity Act and are subject to regulation and supervision by the regulator, the Swedish Energy Markets Inspectorate.

132. On this basis, the Electricity Act mainly regulates matters regarding, and connected with, the transmission of electricity, *inter alia* questions on:

- network concessions, i.e., permit requirements to build and operate certain electricity power lines (*see* paragraphs 235–242);
- TPA rights regarding connection to networks and the use of networks, including principles for the setting of connection tariffs and transmissions tariffs (*see* paragraphs 251–270);
- requirements on the separation of network operation from trading activities and generation of electricity, respectively (*see* paragraphs 247–250);
- balancing of the electricity system, including the overall system responsibility and balancing responsibility (*see* paragraphs 282–289);
- consumer protection with respect to transmission and supply (*see* paragraphs 307–317);
- supervision, including administrative sanctions and penal provisions (*see* paragraphs 318–328).

133. The Electricity Act also contains certain provisions on technical safety issues, which shall not be dealt with herein.

18. *See* Ch. 5 of the introduction *supra* .

134. The Electricity Act is supplemented by a number of ordinances, which are issued by the Government, and by regulations, which are issued primarily by the Swedish Energy Markets Inspectorate. Both the ordinances and the regulations contain detailed provisions concerning various parts of the electricity legislation. The most important of the ordinances supplementing the Electricity Act include:

- the Electricity Ordinance (*Elförordning, SFS 2013:208*), which, among other things, contains detailed provisions regarding network concessions and handling of network concession matters;
- the Ordinance on Exemptions of Concession Requirements (*Förordningen om undantag från kravet på nätkoncession enligt ellagen [1997:857], SFS 2007:215*), which provides that certain high voltage power lines can be constructed without a concession requirement; e.g., so-called internal networks within an industrial area or networks which connect facilities for energy generation, such as wind power turbines;
- the High Voltage Ordinance (*Starkströmsförordningen, SFS 2009:22*) regarding safety regulations, and the obligation to obtain an safety operating permit (*driftstillstånd*) by Swedish National Electricity Safety Board under certain circumstances;
- the Ordinance regarding Reporting of Network Operations (*Förordningen om redovisning av nätverksamhet, SFS 1995:1145*) regarding accounting and book-keeping for network operations, cf. the Electricity Act Chapter 3, section 4;
- the Ordinance regarding Measuring, Calculating and Reporting on Transmitted Electricity (*Förordningen om mätning, beräkning och rapportering av överförd el, SFS 1999:716*) containing instructions on the obligation to meter the quantity of electrical power transmitted and to report the result, cf. the Electricity Act Chapter 3, section 10; and
- the System Responsibility Ordinance (*Förordningen om systemansvaret för el, SFS 1994:1806*) on the appointment of *Svenska Kraftnät* as the authority to be given system responsibility, cf. the Electricity Act Chapter 8, section 1.

135. Directive 2009/72/EC (a part of the EU Third Market Package) containing common rules for the internal market in electricity have been fully implemented in Sweden through the Electricity Act.[19]

§2. Legislation on the Construction and Operation of Electricity Production Plants

136. As regards production (generation) of electricity, which will be the point of departure in this Part I, the applicable regulatory framework largely concerns permit matters with respect to the construction and operation of different kinds of electricity production plants, as well as questions relating to the use of land and water. These rules are not contained in the Electricity Act (apart from concessions for high-voltage power lines). Instead, they are set out in the Environmental Code (*Miljöbalken 1998:808*)

19. Prop. 2008/09:141.

and in special legislation containing specific rules for the energy source in question, such as the Act on Special Provisions on Water Operations (*Lag med särskilda bestämmelser för vattenverksamhet, SFS 1998:812*) (hydro-electrical power plants), and the Nuclear Activities Act (*Kärntekniklagen, SFS 1984:3*) (nuclear power plants).

137. Electricity production from hydropower and nuclear power are further dealt with in paragraphs 151–175 and 176–206, respectively.

138. With respect to electricity generation sources other than hydropower and nuclear power, such as condensing power and cogeneration plants, as well as wind power plants, reference is made to the general overview of environmental and land legislation relevant to the energy law sector, which is provided in Part IV *infra.*

§3. Legislation on Support Mechanisms for Electricity Production from Renewables

139. The Electricity Certificates Act (*SFS 2011:1200*), originally enacted in 2003, constitutes the main support mechanism for production from renewable sources in Sweden. The purpose of the Act is to promote the production of electricity from renewable energy sources by creating a market-based support system. An overview of Electricity Certificates Act, as well as of certain other support mechanisms for renewables, is given in paragraphs 207–228 *infra.*

Chapter 3. Electricity Production

§1. General on Electricity Production from Hydropower and Nuclear Power

I. Hydropower

140. Hydropower is the largest electricity supply source in the country. In 2014, hydropower accounted for approximately 42% (corresponding to 63.9 TWh) of the total electricity production of 146 TWh.[20] Sweden has more than 700 large hydropower stations, whose (individual) effect exceeds 1.5 MW. There are also about 1,200 small hydropower stations, which, in the aggregate, generate approximately 1.5 TWh of energy per year.[21]

141. Under the prevailing energy policy, the long-term objective is to expand hydropower production capacity. However, the development of hydropower must not damage valuable water sources, and that water flow and water level that may be affected by water regulations shall be carried out in such a manner that biological variety is maintained and safeguarded. Furthermore, development of hydropower must not be carried out with respect to rivers and other water courses which are still unregulated, which includes four of the country's largest rivers.[22] Reassessments of old permits to ensure compliance with the EU Water Framework Directive (2000/60/EC) may work to reduce hydropower output. In particular, small hydropower stations could be rendered economically unviable.

II. Nuclear Power

142. Nuclear produced electricity is the second largest electricity supply source in Sweden. There are three operational nuclear power sites in Sweden: *Forsmark*, *Oskarshamn* and *Ringhals*. The nuclear reactors at the forth site, *Barsebäck*, have been taken out of operation. In 2011, the ten nuclear reactors – six Boiling-Water Reactors (BWR) and four Pressurised-Water Reactors (PWR) – in operation on those four sites produced 58 TWh, i.e., almost 40% of the total electricity production.[23] These reactors have a combined installed capacity of 9.4 GWe. During the last decade, most of the remaining reactors have undergone major upgrades and effect increases. As a consequence, more than the 1.2 GWe lost due to the closure of the Barsebäck reactors have been gained by such upgrades.[24] Despite said upgrades, commercial decisions were taken

---

20. The Swedish Energy Markets Inspectorate, EI R 2015:16, p. 18.
21. The Swedish Energy Agency, *The Electricity Market 2002*, p. 15.
22. *See* , e.g., Prop. 2000/01:130.
23. The Swedish Energy Agency; *Energiläget 2012*, pp. 46 et seq.
24. World Nuclear Association, http://www.world-nuclear.org (figure refers to 2010).

in 2015 by the reactor owners (Vattenfall and E.ON, respectively) to close the four oldest of the ten remaining reactors during a period 2016–2020. If indeed such an early closure of these four reactors would occur, Sweden could lose approximately 18% of its domestic electricity production.

143. The first commercial nuclear power reactor was taken into commercial operation in 1972 (Oskarshamn 1). Thereafter, the Swedish nuclear power programme was developed in the 1970s and first half of the 1980s. The construction of new nuclear reactors was prohibited between 1987 and 2010. Under energy policies adopted between 1986 and 2002, the goal was a gradual long-term phase-out of nuclear power from the energy system. As mentioned above, the first step in this process was taken in 1999, when the Barsebäck 1 nuclear power reactor was shut down based on a political decision by the Government based on a special legislation, the Nuclear Phase-Out Act. A second step was taken in 2004, when the Government decided to shut down the Barsebäck 2 nuclear power reactor as of 31 May 2005.

144. However, under the prevailing energy policy, adopted by Parliament in 2009, it was recognized that nuclear power will have an important role in Swedish electricity production for the future *inter alia* as it contributes to low greenhouse gas emissions and Sweden's ambition to further reduce those emissions. Consequently, the Nuclear Phase-Out Act was abolished, and the ban on new construction of nuclear reactors in the Nuclear Activities Act was revoked. The new legislation aims to facilitate a controlled generation change in Sweden's nuclear industry. A fundamental condition governing the design of the new regulatory framework is that a permission to build new reactors will only be given if they replace one of the existing ten reactors and if they are built on existing sites (*see infra*). A further condition is that the construction and operation shall be made without any public subsidies.

145. In addition to the nuclear power plants, certain other nuclear facilities exist in the country. Such nuclear facilities include a central interim storage facility for spent nuclear fuel and other high-level waste from the Swedish reactors (CLAB[25]) located outside the town of Oskarshamn, and a facility for final repository of low and medium-level nuclear waste (SFR[26]) located near the Forsmark nuclear power plant. A final repository for spent nuclear fuel and other high-level waste from the Swedish nuclear reactors is also planned to be constructed outside Forsmark. The licensing process for this facility is in progress.

III. Ownership of Electricity Generation

146. The ownership of the Swedish hydropower and nuclear power plants – and thus electricity production in general – is dominated by a few companies.[27] The Swedish

25. *Centralt mellanlager för använt kärnbränsle.*
26. *Slutförvar för radioaktivt driftavfall.*
27. For an account of ownership of the Swedish electricity production, *see* EI R 2011:07, pp. 33–34.

nuclear power plants are co-owned by Vattenfall AB, E.ON Kärnkraft Sverige AB (as from 2016 Uniper Group, in Sweden Sydkraft AB), and the Fortum-Group.[28]

147. The largest electricity producer in the country is the Vattenfall AB-group, which is owned by the Swedish State. Vattenfall is one of the largest electricity producers in Europe, and accounted for approximately 42% of the total Swedish electricity output in 2010. The company's principal production sources in Sweden are hydropower and nuclear power.

148. The second largest electricity producer is the E.ON Sverige AB-group, which accounted for approximately 19% of the total electricity production in 2010. E.ON Sverige is consolidated by the E.ON AG (Germany), which is the world's largest privately owned energy company. In 2016, *inter alia* the nuclear power and hydropower owning subsidiaries of E.ON were spun off to the Uniper Group (which in Sweden will conduct business under the name Sydkraft AB).

149. The Finnish company Fortum Abp is, since the acquisition of Birka Energi AB in 2002, Sweden's third largest electricity generator (18% of total output). The company's majority owner is the Finnish State (60% of the shares).

150. Other major electricity producers, although much smaller than the above-mentioned companies, are Statkraft Sverige (4% of total electricity production), which is owned by the Norwegian State, and the municipality-owned Skellefteå Kraft AB (2% of total output), whose electricity production system in Sweden is mainly based on hydropower.

§2. Legal Framework for Hydropower

I. General Overview

151. The national legal framework for hydropower is mainly set out in the Environmental Code (*Miljöbalken, SFS 1998:808*) and the Act with Special Provisions on Water Operations (*Lag med särskilda bestämmelser för vattenverksamhet, SFS 1998:812*) (the 'Water Operations Act'). These two acts replaced (from 1999) the 1983 Water Act (*Vattenlagen, SFS 1983:291*), which on its part replaced the 1918 Water Act (*Vattenlagen, SFS 1918:523*). Concerning the Environmental Code and the concept of 'water operations' (*vattenverksamhet*) in general, *see* Part IV, Chapter 2, §6 *infra*.

152. The Water Framework Directive (Directive 2000/60/EC)[29] commits EU Member States to achieve good qualitative and quantitative status of all water bodies by 2015. The objective of achieving good water status should be pursued for each river basin, so that measures in respect of surface water and groundwaters belonging to the same ecological, hydrological and hydrogeological system are coordinated. One important aspect of the Water Framework Directive is the introduction of so-called river basin districts. These areas have been designated, not according to administrative

28. International Energy Agency (IEA), *Energy Policies of IEA Countries, Sweden 2008 Review* 118 (IEA/OECD 2008).
29. Directive 2000/60/EC of the European Parliament and of the Council of 23 Oct. 2000 establishing a framework for Community action in the field of water policy.

or political boundaries, but rather according to the river basin (the spatial catchment area of the river) as a natural geographical and hydrological unit. The Water Framework Directive has been implemented through provisions in Chapter 5 of the Environmental Code and the Ordinance on Management of Water Quality (2004:660), in which the Swedish River Basin Districts (water districts) are defined in detail (cf. Environmental Code, Chapter 5, section 10). For each water district, a County Administrative Board has been appointed to fulfil the tasks as water authority under the Water Framework Directive. Moreover, the Ordinance implements the environmental quality standards (limit values) set forth in Directive 2008/105/EC.[30]

153. On a transnational level, the 1971 Border River Convention between Sweden and Finland[31] as well as the 1929 Water Right Convention between Sweden and Norway are also of practical importance.[32] Under said Conventions – which will not be further dealt with herein – the assessments to be made under national legislation (*inter alia* the Environmental Code) are to some extent replaced by special assessment procedures laid down in the Conventions.[33]

154. The construction and operation of a hydroelectric power plant, dams and other water structures fall within the concept of water operations in the Environmental Code. In order to pursue water operations, each of the following three main conditions must be fulfilled:

(1) The operator must have the right of disposal (*rådighet*) of the water and water area in question (*see* paragraphs 155–163 *infra*).
(2) The operator must have a permit under Chapter 11 of the Environmental Code (*see* paragraphs 164–170 *infra*).
(3) The requirements set out in Chapters 2–4 and Chapter 11 of the Environmental Code must be fulfilled (*see* Part IV, Chapter 2 *infra*).

II. Water Rights

155. Under Swedish law, all water areas (lakes, rivers, etc.), except for the seawater and the waters of the four largest lakes, within 300 metres from the main land (waters outside this distance is in general public waters), form part of real property units and are owned by the respective property owner. Public waters belong to the State.[34]

30. Directive 2008/105/EC of the European Parliament and of the Council of 16 Dec. 2008 on environmental quality standards in the field of water policy, amending and subsequently repealing Council Directives 82/176/EEC, 83/513/EEC, 84/156/EEC, 84/491/EEC, 86/280/EEC and amending Directive 2000/60/EC of the European Parliament and of the Council.
31. SÖ 1971:44.
32. SÖ 1931:10.
33. Further to these Conventions, *see* G. Michanek & C. Zetterberg, *Den svenska miljörätten* 291 (Iustus Förlag 2008).
34. Cf. Act on Delimitation of Public Water Areas (*Lag om gräns mot allmänt vattenområde, SFS 1950:595*).

156. Pursuant to the Water Operations Act (Chapter 2, section 1), the principal rule is that the right to dispose of water and water areas is vested with the owner of the real property to which the water belong – unlike, for example, the system of several Continental European countries, where most lakes and rivers of some importance in general are regarded as public property.

157. In order to pursue water operations, such as the construction and operation of hydroelectric power plants and dams, a fundamental requirement is that the operator has the right to dispose of the water within the area where the operations in question are to be pursued (Water Operations Act, Chapter 2, section 1). As described *supra*, this right of disposal can be based on ownership or rights derived from the owner – such as site leasehold (*tomträtt*), easement (*servitut*) or different forms of rights of user agreements (*nyttjanderättsavtal*) e.g., a ground lease.[35]

158. In some instances, however, statutory rights apply, pursuant to which the right to dispose of water and water areas, as well the right to conduct other measures in connection with water operations, are granted to a person or entity other than the property owner (or the holder of a right of user to the property). Statutory rights which are relevant for the generation of hydropower will be briefly addressed below.

159. First, a person or entity who desires to pursue water operations; which involve: (i) a *water catchment* (*vattentäkt*) for the purposes of (among other things) heat generation for public purposes or (ii) a *water regulation* (*vattenreglering*), has *ipso jure* the requisite water right for this purpose and, hence, the right to use the water on the property of a third party (Water Operations Act, Chapter 2, section 4, items 1–2). By 'water regulation' is meant a manipulation of the flow of a watercourse which is undertaken for the purpose of *another* water operation (Environmental Code, Chapter 11 section 5, paragraph 2). As an example, a power company which owns a falls section with a hydropower plant located downstream the river (and thus have the requisite water right to these falls), has the requisite water right to apply for a water regulation of the source lakes of the river, although these lakes may be situated a long distance from the hydropower operator's property and falls.

160. Second, for the purpose utilizing surface water (i.e., for power generation purposes) or for pursuing a water regulation, the operator may be authorized by the Land and Environmental Court to build structures or take the necessary measures on properties which belong to third parties. An area that is used for this purpose may be compulsorily purchased by the operator if the area is destined to form part of a property to which a hydropower development right is attached (Environmental Code, Chapter 28, section 10, item 4).

161. Third, a person or entity who controls, by way of ownership or easement which is unlimited in time, the major part (i.e., more than 50%) – but not all – of the water power of a fall section in a river, can be granted the right to use the hydropower of the *entire* fall section, i.e., water areas belonging to third parties (Water Operations Act, Chapter 2, section 8).

162. Fourth, under a special rule of the Environmental Code (Chapter 28, section 12), a right to use another person's water structures (e.g., a dam) may be granted by the Environmental Court. This rule stipulates, unless significant inconvenience is caused to the owner of the water structure, that another person or entity may be granted

35. R. Strömberg, *Vattenlagen med kommentarer* 33 (Liber Förlag, 1984).

the right to alter the structure, against payment of the costs for such alteration, or use it (against separate compensation) for his own water operations, or to prevent or mitigate damage caused by his own water operations. The need to use a third party's water structures could, for example, arise with respect to a dam which is used for seasonal regulation of river. Such a dam could be needed to mitigate changes in the flow of the river, which are caused by a hydropower plant located upstream of the dam.[36]

163. Fifth, upon application by a person or entity who desires to generate hydropower from a falls section in a water course owned by another person or entity (other than the State), the Government may grant the applicant to use the falls section by way of expropriation (in the form of ownership or easement right). Such expropriation may, against compensation to the owner for his loss, only take place where this is necessary for the planned development of hydropower (cf. Water Operations Act, Chapter 2, section 9). The main purpose of this rule – which is now considered obsolete – is to prevent undue speculation in hydropower resources.[37]

III. Permits for Water Operations

164. The pursuance of water catchments, water regulations, including the construction and operation of water structures such as hydroelectric power plants and dams, require a permit for water operations under Chapter 11 of the Environmental Code. Permits are assessed and granted by the Land and Environmental Court. Under Chapter 17 of the Environmental Code, the Government – shall, upon the request from the relevant municipal assembly – consider the permissibility of certain large hydropower plants and water regulations, namely hydroelectric power plants designed for an output 20 MW or more, and water regulation facilities with an annual water reservoir capacity of 100 million cubic metre or more (or 10 million cubic metre or more per week), *see also* paragraphs 492–495 *infra*.

165. In general, a number of conditions are attached to a permit for water operations. Common permit conditions with respect to the operation of a hydropower plant or the regulation of the water flow by a dam include *inter alia*: (i) to compensate damage to private property, (ii) to pay annual charges to the State in order to compensate for damages to fishery and to plant out fish in rivers to compensate damage on fishery, and (iii) to compensate other electricity producers or large electricity consumers for their loss of power by allowing them to participate in the production and share the costs of production (joint power).

166. A permit for water operations – such as the exploitation of water for the generation of electricity – is in principle always granted for an indefinite period of time, even though such a permit also can be granted for a defined period in time (Environmental Code, Chapter 16, section 2).

167. A permit or its conditions may be subject of revision after ten years from the date which it gained legal force. In certain cases, a revision can be made within a shorter period of time, *inter alia* for safety reasons (such as dam safety) or if the activity

36. Cf. R. Strömberg, *Vattenlagen med kommentarer* 123 (Liber Förlag 1984).
37. R. Strömberg, *Vattenlagen med kommentarer* 45–46 (Liber Förlag 1984).

causes any significant damage which was not anticipated when the permit was granted. In practice however, few permits concerning hydropower (generally granted under pre-Environmental Code legislation) have up-to-date been subject to revision under the Code.[38] Moreover, a revision – which may entitle the operator to compensation for losses – must not impose conditions or other rules that are so intrusive that the activity no longer can be pursued or is significantly hampered (Environmental Code, Chapter 24, section 5). With respect to legal force and revision of permits, *see also* paragraphs 524–527 *infra*.

168. Under special circumstances a permit may be revoked (in part or in whole), for example, if the operator has manifestly neglected his maintenance obligations with respect to a water structure, e.g., a hydroelectric power plant or a dam (Environmental Code, Chapter 24, section 3).

169. If a permit to operate and maintain a water structure (e.g., a dam or power plant) is revoked, the person or entity who is responsible for maintenance of the structure (in general the operator) will be liable to dismantle and remove – or pay for such measures – the water structure in question and, in addition, take any measures that are necessary to prevent and mitigate damage caused by the decommissioning/removal (Environmental Code, Chapter 24, section 4).

170. In view of the fact that many existing permits for hydropower and dams have been issued under old legislation (mainly the 1918 Water Act), in which few or no conditions concerning environmental protection are attached, the Government has initiated a review of the Swedish water legislation aiming at a more effective implementation of the fundamental environmental law principles (e.g., the polluter pays principle and the application best available technique) within the legal framework for water operations.[39]

IV. Right to Compensation upon Revision of Permits

171. If the State, e.g., for the purpose of improving the environment or fishery, requests a review of the conditions for a permit and the Environmental Court's decision on this issue leads to a reduction of power, the permit holder is entitled to compensation from the State for the loss of power to the extent the loss exceeds a level prescribed by law or by the Court. Regarding permits under the 1918 Water Act, the level is set to 5% of the production value, whereas the level for permits under the 1983 Water Act and the Environmental Code varies between 5% and 20% of the production value, prescribed by the Court for each power plant when the permit was issued.[40]

172. It could be noted that there is no right to compensation if the revision is made in order to improve dam safety.

---

38. Dir. 2012:29, p. 7.
39. Dir. 2012:29.
40. Environmental Code, Ch. 31, s. 22 and Promulgation Act to the Environmental Code, s. 39.

V. Water Regulation Associations

173. The storage of water in basins and the regulation of the water flow by dams often have a significant value to several hydropower plants downstream the river. Therefore, the water legislation provides that the owners of such plants should cooperate in water regulation associations (*vattenregleringssamfälligheter*) in order to share the costs. Each plant owner contributes to the costs in proportion to his benefit of the regulation (*see* Water Operations Act, Chapter 5).

VI. Responsibility for Dam Safety

174. The owner of a dam (or a person or entity that have been designated by the Water Court or the Environmental Court to be responsible for the maintenance of the dam), is responsible for the safety of the dam. The owner is also liable for damage caused by dam failure. The liability is strict, i.e., the damage must not to have been caused intentionally or by negligence (Environmental Code, Chapter 11, section 18).

VII. Supervision of Hydropower Plants

175. The supervision of hydropower plants, dams and water regulations in accordance with the Environmental Code is exercised by the County Administrative Board in the county where the plant or facility is located. The supervision includes primarily the task to ensure that the provisions in the Environmental Code as well as permits and permits conditions stipulated in water judgments pursuant to the Code (or older legislation) are complied with by the operators.

As regards supervision in general under the Environmental Code, *see* paragraphs 556–559 *infra*.

§3. Legal Framework for Nuclear Power

I. General Overview

176. The following statutes constitute the main legislative framework with respect to nuclear power:

- The Nuclear Activities Act (*Kärntekniklag, SFS 1984:3*), which contains the main principles of the regulatory system.
- The Radiation Protection Act (*Strålskyddslag, SFS 1988:220*) which contains general provisions on safety measures relating to ionizing and non-ionizing radiation.

- The Nuclear Liability Act (*Atomansvarighetslag, SFS 1968:45*), which is based on international conventions[41] and deals with nuclear third-party liability. The Nuclear Liability Act will be repealed and replaced by the Act on Liability and Compensation due to Radiological Accidents (*Lag om ansvar och ersättning vid radiologiska olyckor, SFS 2010:950*). At the time of writing, the latter Act has not yet entered into force.
- The Environmental Code (*see* further Part IV, Chapter 2), which is generally applicable with respect to nuclear installations and which contains special permit provisions covering nuclear reactors and other nuclear installations.
- Provisions regarding financing of nuclear fuel waste and decommissioning of nuclear reactors are set forth in the Act on Financing of Management of Residual Products from Nuclear Activities (*SFS 2006:647*).

177. The Radiation Safety Authority (*Strålsäkerhetsmyndigheten*) is the main regulatory authority for the Swedish nuclear power plants and other nuclear installations. The Radiation Safety Authority is the central national authority for protection against ionizing and non-ionizing radiation.

II. Safety and Permit Requirements for Nuclear Installations

178. The principal regulatory provisions with respect to Sweden's nuclear installations are set out in the Nuclear Activities Act, which regulates 'nuclear activities'. The Act is supplemented by the Nuclear Activities Ordinance (1984:14). The Radiation Safety Authority has been given the task to issue detailed regulations regarding all aspects of safety matters in nuclear facilities. These regulations – which contain the concrete legal nuclear safety framework – are to a large extent based on, or take into consideration, international conventions and standards as well as applicable EU directives. The regulations apply to both physical protection of nuclear facilities and the personal protection of workers and the general public in connection with activities that involve ionizing radiation. The regulations are published by the Radiation Safety Authority in the series SSMFS.[42]

179. The Nuclear Activities Act defines 'nuclear activities' as the erection, possession or operation of a nuclear plant, the acquisition, possession, transfer, processing, transport or other handling of nuclear substances or nuclear waste, the import of nuclear substances or nuclear waste, as well as the export from Sweden of nuclear waste (section 1).

180. The basic provisions of the Nuclear Activities Act provide that nuclear activities shall be pursued so that both safety requirements and Sweden's international non-proliferation obligations (*inter alia* the Treaty on the Non-Proliferation of Nuclear Weapons) are fulfilled. (section 3).

181. All nuclear activities are subject to a permit requirement under the Nuclear Activities Act. Such a permit is decided and issued by the Government or the Radiation Safety Authority.

41. The Paris Convention and the Brussels Supplementary Convention.
42. *Strålsäkerhetsmyndighetens föreskrifter*.

182. A permit can be revoked if the permit holder does not comply with permit conditions or the provisions in the Nuclear Activities Act on pursuance of research and development (*see infra*) and extraordinary safety grounds are at hand, *or* otherwise if extraordinary safety grounds arise (section 15).

183. Under the Nuclear Activities Act, the permit holder is solely responsible for the safety of the nuclear activity that the permit covers. The permit holder is also responsible for ensuring safe handling and final storage of nuclear waste arising from the nuclear activity in question and the safe decommissioning and dismantling of plants in which nuclear operations no longer are conducted (section 10). These obligations will continue to apply also in the situation where a permit under the Nuclear Activities Act has been revoked, or if the right to operate a nuclear reactor has been terminated pursuant to the, now repealed, Nuclear Power Phase-Out Act (*SFS 1997:1320*) (section 14). Moreover, the licence holder must conduct research and development work in relation to nuclear waste and the decommissioning of nuclear plants (sections 11–12).

184. In addition, certain provisions of the Environmental Code are applicable in the assessment of permit matters under the Nuclear Activities Act,[43] namely the general rules of consideration (Chapter 2) and the provisions on environmental quality standards (Chapter 5, section 3). Further, an Environmental Impact Assessment (EIA) pursuant to the procedure prescribed under Chapter 6 of the Environmental Code shall be conducted in licence matters under the Nuclear Activities Act (*see also* paragraphs 509–513 *infra*).

185. The construction of all new major[44] nuclear facilities, as well as the decommissioning and dismantling of nuclear power plants and other nuclear reactors, are subject to a permit requirement under Chapter 9 of the Environmental Code.[45] For these kinds of activities, the permit is issued by a regional Land and Environmental Court, who may attach conditions to the permit (*see also* paragraphs 518–523 *infra*). Nevertheless, the *permissibility* for new nuclear (major) installations is decided by the Government under the Environmental Code. This permissibility decision cannot be overruled by the Land and Environmental Court. Thus, the crucial licensing decisions – under both Nuclear Activities Act and the Environmental Code – for new nuclear facilities are taken by the Government.

186. In spite of the above, the Government can only permit the construction of new nuclear facilities which have been approved by the appropriate municipal council of the municipality where the activities are intended to be pursued – i.e., a municipal veto. However, as regards facilities for intermediate storage or final disposal of nuclear material or waste, this veto does not apply if the activities, from a national perspective, are of exceptional importance. Such facilities may therefore be permitted by the Government even if the municipal council does not approve, unless: (a) a more appropriate site for the activity is deemed to exist, or (b) if an appropriate site has been

---

43. Cf. Nuclear Activities Act, s. 5 b.
44. According to the Environmental Code, Ch. 17, Sec. the Government must assess the permissibility (according to the Environmental Code) of all new nuclear facilities which are subject to Government assessment under the Nuclear Activities Act (i.e., major installations), as well as facilities for mining of uranium or other materials that can be used for the extraction of nuclear fuel.
45. These provisions are based on the EIA-Directive 2011/92/EU.

designated in another municipality which is likely to approve the site (Environmental Code, Chapter 17, section 6).

III. Licensing of New Nuclear Reactors

187. The existing Swedish nuclear reactors were taken into operation from the beginning of the 1970s until the mid-1980s. Following a 1980 referendum and the Chernobyl disaster in 1986, Parliament decided in 1987 to amend the Nuclear Activities Act to prohibit the issuance of licences for new nuclear power reactors. In 1998, the Act on Nuclear Power Phase-Out (*SFS 1997:1320*) was enacted.[46] Under this legislation, the Government was given a mandate to decide that the right to operate an individual nuclear power reactor for the purpose of generation of nuclear energy would cease to apply at the point in time stipulated by the Government. Based on this legislation, the Government decided to close down two existing nuclear reactors, the *Barsebäck 1* and the *Barsebäck 2*, which were taken out of operation in 1999 and 2005, respectively.[47]

188. Based on a political agreement in 2009, Parliament repealed the following year the prohibition to construct new nuclear reactors in the Nuclear Activities Act. New legislation was adopted allowing the replacement of the existing nuclear reactors with new nuclear reactors at existing sites, starting from 1 January 2011.[48] Under prevailing rules, the main prerequisites for construction and operation of new nuclear power reactors are the following.

189. The Government examines the permissibility for new nuclear reactors under both the Nuclear Activities Act and the Environmental Code[49] (*see infra*). The Government can grant a licence[50] for a new nuclear power reactor only if the new reactor is intended to: (i) replace an existing nuclear power reactor that has produced energy after 31 May 2005 and which will be permanently shut down[51] when the new reactor is taken into commercial operation, and (ii) be constructed at a site where a nuclear power reactor has been in operation for producing energy after 31 May 2005

46. For an more detailed account of the Nuclear Phase-Out Act and connected questions, *see* Wiwen-Nilsson, Håkansson & Wärnsby, Energy Law – *Monograph Sweden, in International Encyclopaedia of Laws* 64–66 (Kluwer Law International 2005).
47. The decision to close down Barsebäck 1 prompted a legal dispute with the owner of the reactor (Barsebäck Kraft AB and Sydkraft AB), and the matter was *inter alia* referred to judicial review in the Supreme Administrative Court (RÅ 1999 ref. 76). After having decided to postpone the closure of the reactor (RÅ 1998 not 93), the Court ruled in 1999, that the Government's decision was lawful (RÅ 1999. ref. 76). For a detailed account of the so-called *Barsebäck* case, *see inter alia* Nergelius, *Förvaltningsprocess,normprövning och Europarätt* 72 et seq. and 102 et seq (Nordstedts Juridik 2000), and C. Lundblad & M. Wärnsby, 'Proportionalitetsprincipen inom förvaltningsrätten efter Barsebäcksdomen', Europarättslig tidskrift, No 2, 2000, 209 and a commentary to the EIA question is given by J. Ebbesson, 'Miljökonsekvensbedömningar när kärnkraftverk avvecklas?', Juridisk Tidskrift 1999–2000, 895.
48. *See* Prop. 2009/10:172.
49. This is in spite of the fact that the license under the Environmental Code is granted by an Environmental Court.
50. Subject to the 'municipal veto', *see* para. 186 *supra* .
51. It is not required that the old reactor has been decommissioned, *see* Prop. 2009/10:172, p. 52.

(Nuclear Activities Act, section 5 b and Environmental Code, Chapter 17, section 6 a). Hence, it is possible to replace existing reactors with new ones at the existing sites. The replacement reactor does not necessarily have to be constructed at the same site as the one to be replaced. If, for instance, one reactor in Forsmark is closed, the replacement reactor could be constructed at the existing nuclear sites in Oskarshamn or Ringhals.[52] However, the reactors that have been closed according to the Nuclear Phase-Out Act (*see supra*) – i.e., the Barsebäck 1 and Barsebäck 2 reactors – must not be re-started (Nuclear Activities Act, section 15 a).

IV. Transnational Consultation Obligations

190. The licensing of new nuclear facilities in Sweden may be subject to international consultation and information requirements. According to the *Espoo Convention* (or the EIA-Convention),[53] private parties in are entitled to take part in other countries' decision procedures regarding the EIA for operations that have cross-border impacts on the environment. Further, under a *Joint Agreement on Information between the Scandinavian Countries* of 1976, the Radiation Safety Authority has a duty to inform the corresponding authorities in Denmark, Finland and Norway if, among other things, licences are granted to the operation of nuclear facilities or changes are made in the licences conditions.[54] Also according to *Article 37 of the Euratom Treaty*, each Member State must inform the Commission of plans to store nuclear waste in order for the Commission to assess if such planned activities could cause contamination of water, ground or air in another Member State.

V. Trade in Nuclear Substances and Equipment

191. As stated in paragraphs 178–186 *supra*, trade in nuclear substances and equipment governed by the Nuclear Activities Act. The Act's definition of nuclear activities includes, *inter alia*, the import and export of nuclear substances and waste. Consequently, such activities are subject to the Act's permit and safety provisions.

192. Under the Nuclear Activities Act, it is prohibited to import spent nuclear fuel or other nuclear waste from another country for the purpose of final disposal or intermediate storage in Sweden, without a special permit from the Government (or SSM). Certain exceptions exist, *inter alia* with respect to spent fuel from research reactors (cf. section 5a and 5b).

193. The Ordinance on Nuclear Activities contains detailed provisions for the import and export of nuclear substances and equipment to and from Sweden. Such

52. Prop. 2009/10:172, p. 30.
53. Convention on Environmental Impact Assessment in a Transboundary Context, Espoo, 25 Feb. 1991.
54. Ministerial note between Sweden, Denmark, Finland and Norway 15 Nov. 1976 regarding guidelines for information in safety matters concerning nuclear facilities at the borders between Denmark, Finland, Norway and Sweden.

measures are subject to a licence or notification requirement depending on how the substance and material in question is categorized in the Ordinance.

VI. Radiation Protection

194. Provisions regarding the protection of human health, animals and the environment from ionizing and non-ionizing radiation are laid down in the Radiation Protection Act (cf. sections 1–2). In addition, the Environmental Code is applicable with respect to activities which are capable of causing ionizing and non-ionizing radiation; *see* Chapter 9, section 1, item 3.

195. Under the Radiation Protection Act, the handling of radioactive substances or equipment which may generate or emit ionizing radiation requires a permit (section 20). As the principal rule, a permit under the Radiation Protection Act is not required if the relevant activity is covered by a permit granted under the Nuclear Activities Act (section 23). Certain provisions of the Environmental Code are applicable in the assessment of permit matters under the Radiation Protection Act (section 22a).

196. The Radiation Protection Act also imposes a number of safety and precautionary obligations on a person or entity, who manufactures, imports, sells or handles substances or devices that are capable of generating or emitting radiation. Certain obligations of this kind also apply for those who install or conduct service work with respect to such devices. Further, the Act contains provisions on the handling of waste from radiation activities (sections 9–14).

VII. Nuclear Liability

197. Sweden is a party *inter alia* to the following international conventions on nuclear liability:

- the 1960 Paris Convention on Third Party Liability in the Field of Nuclear Energy (as amended by two 1964 and 1982 Supplementary Protocols[55]); and
- the 1963 Brussels Convention Supplementary to the Paris Convention (as amended by the 1964 and 1982 Supplementary Protocols[56]).

198. These conventions have been transformed into Swedish law through the Nuclear Liability Act. Certain main provisions of the Nuclear Liability Act are briefly summarized below.

199. Pursuant to the Nuclear Liability Act, the operator of a nuclear installation (i.e., the permit holder under the Nuclear Activities Act), which has caused a nuclear incident, has a strict and absolute liability to compensate those who have suffered personal injury or damage to property resulting from the nuclear incident (sections 5 and 11). At the time of writing, the amount of the operator's liability is limited to 300

55. SÖ 1968:17. *See also* SÖ 1968:18, 1968:20 and 1983:31.
56. SÖ 1968:19. *See also* SÖ 1964:20 and 1983:32.

million Special Drawing Rights (SDR) per incident, corresponding to approximately SEK 3 billion (section 17).

200. Each operator of nuclear installations is obliged to have insurance, approved by the Government, covering the above-mentioned liability limit (i.e., 300 million SDR). The insurance requirement does not apply for the State (sections 22–27).

201. Under the Nuclear Liability Act, compensation can be granted in excess of the compensation amounts that are obtainable under the Paris Convention and the Brussels Supplementary Convention. If the compensation payable under said Conventions does not constitute full compensation to cover the damage, the State may compensate those who have suffered such damage by a maximum amount of SEK 6 billion per incident. Such additional compensation is available only in relation to a nuclear damage suffered in Sweden, Denmark, Finland or Norway, or in the territory of any other party to the Brussels Supplementary Convention, provided that such other country has made a mutual compensation undertaking for damage that have arisen in Sweden (section 31 a).

202. In 2010, the Swedish Parliament approved Sweden's accession to the 2004 Protocol amending the Paris Convention and the Supplementary Convention.[57] Under the 2004 Protocol, the minimum level of nuclear liability for the operator was raised and the convention states are now allowed to introduce an unlimited liability for the operator of a nuclear installation. Once the 2004 Protocol enters into force between the convention states,[58] the old Nuclear Liability Act will be repealed and replaced by new legislation on the national level: the Act on Liability and Compensation due to Radiological Accidents (*SFS 2010:950*). The new Act – which should be viewed in the light of the new legislation allowing new nuclear reactors to be built in replacement of old reactors (*see supra*) – is based on the same principles of channelling of the nuclear liability to the operator of a nuclear installation as are set forth in the Paris-Brussels Conventions and the Nuclear Liability Act (*see supra*). However, an important novelty is the introduction of an unlimited liability for the operator of nuclear facilities (Act on Liability and Compensation due to Radiological Accidents, sections 15 and 27). Although an unlimited liability does not constitute a guarantee that the injured parties can always receive full compensation for damage suffered, the Swedish legislator has held that there is an ethical and symbolical value in adhering as far as possible to the 'polluter pays principle' which is fundamental in environmental law.[59]

203. Moreover, under the new nuclear liability regime, an operator of a nuclear facility in Sweden will be obliged to have and maintain a liability insurance or some other financial security that corresponds to EUR 700 million and that will always cover the liability to pay compensation under the 2004 Protocol Amending the Paris Convention. An additional insurance or security obligation will apply to operators of nuclear reactors. Hence, the operator of a nuclear reactor that is in operation to extract nuclear

57. 2009/10:CU29 and rskr. 2009/10:360.
58. At the time of writing (January 2013), the 2004 Protocol amending the Paris Convention and the Supplementary Convention has still not entered into force as it is subject to ratification in certain other states. The new nuclear liability legislation enters into force on the date decided by the Swedish Government, subsequent to the ratification of the Protocol by the required number of states.
59. Prop. 2009/10:173, s. 53.

energy shall be obliged to ensure that funds corresponding to a total of EUR 1,200 million are available for every accident in order to compensate injured parties entitled to damages (the Act on Liability and Compensation due to Radiological Accidents, section 30).

VIII. Financing of Radioactive Waste Management

204. Pursuant to the Nuclear Activities Act, the responsibility for the management of radioactive waste lies with the permit holder carrying out the activities which produce the waste. The financing of the final disposal of spent nuclear fuel and nuclear waste, as well as the decommissioning of nuclear reactors, is regulated by the Act on Financing of Management of Residual Products from Nuclear Activities (SFS 2006:647). This Act requires the holder of a licence for a nuclear reactor or another nuclear installation to pay an annual fee and make available adequate financial guarantees to a state-controlled fund, the Nuclear Waste Fund. The fund is managed by a Governmental authority, the Board of the Nuclear Waste Fund (Act on Financing of Management of Residual Products from Nuclear Activities, section 6).

205. The amount of the fee is calculated according to the energy output of each nuclear facility and is determined as a fixed amount for each delivered kWh. The fee can also be determined as a fixed amount, for example, if the fee is paid by a licensee who no longer delivers nuclear energy. The size of the fee varies annually and among the nuclear facilities. If the fees accumulated in the fund are insufficient to cover estimated costs – which at present is the case – each licensee must present a guarantee to the state for the costs the fee is intended to cover (Act on Financing of Management of Residual Products from Nuclear Activities, section 9). The Radiation Safety Authority calculates and proposes the annual fees and financial guarantees, which are ultimately determined and approved by the Government.[60]

206. The Studsvik Act (*Studsviklagen, SFS 1988:1597*) regulates fees and reimbursements to cover the expenses for managing nuclear waste from old experimental nuclear facilities, in particular the facilities at Studsvik, the Ågesta reactor and the uranium mine in Ranstad. According to the Studsvik Act, a special fee is levied on the permit holder for this purpose. The Studsvik Act will cease to apply as of 2018.

60. By the end of 2015, the total fond capital was SEK 59,284 million, whereas the fee was on average SEK 0.004 per kWh (*see* the Annual Report 2015 of the Board of the Nuclear Waste Fund).

§4. Support Mechanisms for Renewable Energy Sources

I. Directive 2009/28/EC and Support Mechanisms in General

207. In 2009, the Directive 2009/28/EC on the promotion of the use of energy from renewable sources (the Renewable Energy Directive) was adopted.[61] The aim of the Renewable Energy Directive is to promote the use of renewable energy in all sectors by the most important principle of having the energy price reflect production costs and cost of use including environmental, social and health costs. The Directive contains binding national targets for renewable energy, including binding minimum targets for the transport sector. For the EU as a whole, the Renewable Energy Directive aims to increase the share of renewable energy to 20% by 2020, compared with 8.5% in 2005. The binding target for Sweden in 2020 is 49%, which is an increase of over 9% points compared to the 2005 level.

208. The Directive contains a number of measures to reduce barriers and promote the use of renewable energy. It requires Member States to adopt national action plans for the fulfilment of the target for 2020. It contains control provisions as well as calculation bases for the targets and contains sustainability criteria to avoid biofuels to be developed at the expense of biodiversity. The Renewable Energy Directive has been implemented into Swedish law *inter alia* through the Act on Sustainability Criteria (*Lag om hållbarhetskriterier, SFS 2010:598*).

209. Intergovernmental cooperation is also an important aspect of the Directive. Further, it sets new requirements for the electricity market by imposing requirements of a guarantee of origin for electricity and heating from renewable sources as well as guaranteed grid access for electricity from renewable energy sources.

210. In line with the Directive, Sweden has decided to continue to apply economic instruments in taxation together with three national action plans: one for a fossil fuel independent transport sector, one for increased energy efficiency and one for promoting renewable energy. The vision for Sweden is to have zero net emissions of GHG in year 2050.[62]

211. The Swedish Government provides support to renewable energy sources mainly through tax incentives and a market-orientated support mechanism, the so-called electricity certificates system.[63] There is also a system for subsidizing solar energy in force.

---

61. Directive 2009/28/EC of the European Parliament and of the Council of 23 Apr. 2009 on the promotion of the use of energy from renewable sources and amending and subsequently repealing Directives 2001/77/EC and 2003/30/EC.
62. Prop. 2008/09:162 and Prop. 2008/09:163.
63. Another market-based support mechanism – however not specifically designed to promote renewable energy sources – is the Emissions Trading Scheme (ETS).

II. The Electricity Certificates Act

212. In the 2002 energy policy bill, the main principles of a system based on tradable certificates aimed at supporting electricity production from renewables were introduced. On this basis, a government bill on electricity certificates and the Electricity Certificates Act were adopted by Parliament in 2003. The former act was replaced by a new Electricity Certificates Act in 2012 (*Lag om elcertifikat, SFS 2011:1200*).[64] The Act is supplemented by the Electricity Certificates Ordinance (2011:1480), which contains detailed provisions of the certificates system.[65]

213. The purpose of the Electricity Certificates Act is to encourage the production of electricity from renewable energy sources, rather than from conventional sources, by creating a market-based support system.[66]

214. Moreover, the electricity certificate system is a measure for the fulfilment of the renewable energy target of an increase by 30 TWh renewable energy from the 2002 level until 2020. As of 1 January 2012, Sweden and Norway have a joint electricity certificates market, and the common target of the two countries is to achieve an expansion of renewable energy production to an additional yearly production of 13.2 TWh between 2012 and 2020.

215. In 2011, the generation from renewable energy sources and peat covered by the quota obligation was 19.8 TWh, which is an increase of 13.3 TWh compared to the 2002 level.

216. Producers of electricity, which must be approved by the Swedish Energy Agency, will receive one electricity certificate for each MWh of renewable electricity produced, cf. the Electricity Certificates Act, Chapter 2, section 1 and Chapter 3, section 2. The certificate constitutes an electronic record registered in a database kept by the operator of the main grid, *Svenska Kraftnät.*

217. Renewable energy sources, which qualifies for certificates under the Act, are:

- wind power;
- solar power;
- wave energy;
- geothermal energy;
- hydropower with a capacity not exceeding 1.5 MW (i.e., small-scale hydropower);
- biofuels as specified in the Ordinance (2011:1480) on electricity certificates; and
- peat in power and heating plants.

218. New facilities that have become operational after the introduction of the certificate system are entitled to obtain certificates for a period of fifteen years, however at the longest until 2035. Facilities built before the system was introduced are in most cases entitled to certificates until 2012 or 2014. According to the new Electricity Certificates Act from 2012, the Swedish Energy Agency shall determine the period

64. Prop. 2010/11:155.
65. *See also* the Swedish Energy Agency's regulations and general advice on electricity certificates (STEMFS 2011:4).
66. SOU 2001:77, Prop. 2002/03:40, pp. 1–2.

for allotment of certificates when a facility is approved for obtaining certificates, meaning that the owner will know when the period of allotment will cease. The periods will normally be fifteen years.[67]

219. The demand for electricity certificates are created by the so-called quota obligation. The quota obligation means that purchasers on the electricity market, primarily electricity suppliers, are required to purchase certificates corresponding to a certain proportion of their electricity sales or use. The sizes of quota obligations are set by the Electricity Certificates Act in Sweden, and the correspondent legislation in Norway – as Sweden and Norway have a joint electricity certificate system.

220. The parties having a quota obligation under the Electricity Certificates Act are obliged to purchase a certain number of certificates in proportion to their respective supply or use of electricity. These actors on the market are:

- Suppliers of electricity.
- Electricity consumers of electricity produced by themselves if the amount of consumed electricity exceed 60 MWh per year and has been produced in a facility with an installed effect exceeding 50 kW.
- Electricity consumers of imported electricity or of electricity purchased on the Nordic Power Exchange.
- Electricity intensive industries registered by the Swedish Energy Agency.

221. A party having quota obligation must register with the Swedish Energy Agency within two weeks from the date when the managing of the quota obligation started. Before 1 March each year, the supplier must submit a report to the Swedish Energy Agency showing the invoiced electricity during the previous year. No later than on 1 April each year, the supplier must have at its disposal on its certificate account the number of electricity certificates required to meet the quota of the relevant sale of electricity or use of electricity during the year, cf. the Electricity Certificate Act, Chapter 4, section 2. In case this duty is not fulfilled, the party will be charged a penalty amounting to 150% of the average certificate price for the relevant period of time per (omitted) certificate, Chapter 6, section 1.

222. It may also be noted that commercial trade in electricity certificates requires a licence under the Swedish Securities Trading Act (*Lagen om handel med finansiella instrument, SFS 1991:980*). However, the mere management of a quota obligation by a supplier or another party (as described *supra*) is not subject to such a licence requirement.

III. Subsidies for Solar Cells

223. In addition to small-scale hydropower and biomass, wind power and solar power are the two technologies that, at present, are deemed to have the major development potentials of the renewable energy sources that could be used in Sweden.

224. Wind power plants for electricity production have been subject to a generous state introduction support scheme and have efficiently contributed to an expansion of

67. The Electricity Certificates Act, Ch. 2, s. 7.

wind power in Sweden.[68] However, at the time of writing (January 2013), the subsidies for wind power, except for electricity certificates (*see supra*), have been phased out and there is currently no such support for the installation of new wind power turbines.

225. Since 2009, Sweden has a state-aid scheme in place for the installation of solar panels. The aim is to create a market for solar cells systems in Sweden in order to contribute to the change of the energy system and industrial development in the field of energy techniques. The objective is also to increase the number of suppliers and users of solar cells in Sweden, contribute to decreased costs for the systems and increase the annual electricity production from solar cells by at least 2.5 GWh during the duration of the scheme.

226. The aid for solar cell system is regulated in the Ordinance on State Aid for Solar Cells (*SFS 2009:689*). The aid covers all types of actors, companies and public organizations as well as private persons. The subsidy may also be granted to solar electricity/solar heating-hybrids, i.e., a system generating both electricity and heating.[69]

227. As of 1 January 2015, the subsidies can amount to maximum 30% of the costs (20% for private individuals) and may not exceed SEK 1.2 million per system. In its budget for 2016, the Government has allocated SEK 1.4 billion for solar cells subsidies to be distributed over a period of four years.[70]

228. Applications for subsidies are submitted to the County Administrative Boards (*länsstyrelse*), which also are the authorities administrating and deciding on the granting of solar cell subsidies.

IV. Tax Reduction for Microgeneration of Renewable Electricity

229. As of 1 January 2015, it is possible to receive a tax reduction for microgeneration of renewable electricity (typically solar cells and small wind power plants). The tax reduction equals SEK 0.6 per kWh for all electricity fed in to the electricity network, however not exceeding SEK 18,000 per each year.

V. Act on Energy Audits in Large Enterprises

230. The Act on Energy Audits in Large Enterprises (*Lag om energikartläggning i stora företag*, *SFS 2014:266*) requires all large companies (as defined in the Act) to conduct an energy audit of their operations every fourth year. Detailed provisions concerning the audit are set forth in the Ordinance on Energy Audits in Large Enterprises (*SFS 2014:347*) and in a regulation by the Energy Agency (*STEMFS 2014:2*).

---

68. In 2012, approximately 7 TWh wind power energy was produced in Sweden, to be compared to 0.45 TWh in 2000.
69. Ordinance on State Aid for Solar Cells (*SFS 2009:689*).
70. www.energimyndigheten.se.

Chapter 4. Transmission of Electricity

§1. The Swedish Electricity Network

231. The national grid was originally constructed for the purpose of transmitting electricity generated from hydropower from the surplus areas in the northern parts of Sweden to the southern areas of the country. The network of power lines, which transmits electricity from power stations to consumers, is classified into three levels, the national grid, regional networks and local networks. The national grid includes lines of 220 kV and 400 kV and the majority of the links to the neighbouring countries. The regional networks, comprising lines of voltages of 70 kV–130 kV, in rare cases 220 kV, transmit electricity from the national grid to local networks and in certain cases to users with a high consumption of electricity such as major industrial plants and local network utilities. From the local networks, which normally operate at a maximum of 20 kV, in the distribution area electricity is transformed to the normal domestic voltage of 380/220 volt.[71]

232. There are certain limitations in the north-south connections which limits the power that can be transmitted. The most important bottleneck is between northern and central Sweden limiting the power that can be transmitted to between 6,700 and 7,000 MW. Another bottleneck is between central and southern Sweden. The link between southern Norway and Sweden (Hasle) is also an important bottleneck. When consumption in the Oslo region is high, the capacity on the link to Sweden is substantially reduced.

233. Bottlenecks in Sweden are handled by counter-purchases. If the transmission capacity of the national grid is insufficient for transmitting electricity to meet the actual requirements of the customer, *Svenska Kraftnät* applies a counter-purchase. This reduces the physical energy flow on the grid, without the trade or users being affected.

234. In 2010, the European Commission adopted a decision[72] – based on Article 9 of Regulation 1/2003 on the implementation of the (former) EC Treaty's competition rules – to the effect that Sweden must modify the managing of transmission limitations in the Swedish electricity network. This decision was the result of a complaint by a Danish energy undertaking. The Commission held that the model in use until then (reduction of capacity and counter trading, *see infra*) was discriminatory against foreign operators and in conflict with the efforts to establish a common European electricity market. As a consequence of this decision, *Svenska Kraftnät* has (as of 1 November 2011) divided Sweden into four bidding areas (price areas), with the following designations:

- the Luleå bidding area (SE1);
- the Sundsvall bidding area (SE 2);

71. For a detailed account of the Swedish electricity transmission network, *see* e.g. The Energy Markets Inspectorate, Report EI R 2011:9, pp. 17 et seq.
72. Commission decision IP/10/425, 14 Apr. 2010.

- the Stockholm bidding area (SE 3);
- the Malmö bidding area (SE 4).

This separation indicates areas in the country where reinforcement of the electricity network and increase of generation capacity are required to achieve a better match with electricity consumption and in order to reduce the need for long-distance electricity transmission.[73] As a result of this division in bidding areas, the price of the commodity (electricity) will during certain periods (i.e., not always) differ between the different bidding areas, typically resulting in a relative price increase in the south compared to the northern areas. Such differences are likely to remain until new transmission or generation capacity has been established at the crucial locations.

§2. Network Concessions

I. General

235. High-voltage power lines may only be constructed and operated by a person or entity that has been granted a network concession (licence) pursuant to the Electricity Act. For the purpose of the Act, construction includes land drilling, wood clearing and similar activities necessary to clear the way for a power line (Chapter 2, section 1).

236. There are two types of network concessions under the Electricity Act, *see* Chapter 2, section 2. The first type, a network concession for a line, is a concession for a certain power line of a principally defined length. This type of concession is mainly used for lines in the regional network. The second type, a network concession for an area, is a concession for power lines within a certain defined area. This type of concession is granted for the right to build and operate local networks.[74]

237. The Energy Markets Inspectorate has been authorized by the Government to grant network concessions for power lines used for transmission within Sweden. As a main rule, private entities are not able to obtain a network concession for cross-border power lines. Such concessions are reserved to the operator in charge of the national grid, currently the state utility *Svenska Kraftnät*. However, should the power line be of minor importance with respect to the aggregate cross-border transmission network such concession may be granted also to private entities by the Government (the Electricity Act, Chapter 2, section 10).

II. Conditions for Granting of Network Concessions

238. A network concession may be granted only if the installation is considered appropriate (*lämplig*) from a public interest point of view. The purpose is to prevent construction of lines which are unnecessary from national economy point of view, i.e.,

73. The Energy Markets Inspectorate, Report EI R 2011:9, pp. 19–20.
74. Prop. 1996/97:136 p. 120.

construction of new lines in areas with adequate transmission capacity or where they cause unreasonable damage or inconvenience to third parties.[75]

239. A line concession will not be granted if it is incompatible with a detailed development plan or area regulations under the Planning and Building Act[76] (the Electricity Act, Chapter 2, section 8). There are also environmental issues that must be considered. The person applying for a line concession must *inter alia* conduct an EIA in accordance with Chapter 6 of the Environmental Code.[77] None of these planning and environmental prerequisites apply to a concession for a region. As such concessions include the right to construct and use a network within a defined area, the legislator has for practical purposes deemed it impossible to apply the same conditions as for a line concession.[78] As regards concessions for an area, the Electricity Act merely provides that the area in question must be appropriate for network operations (Chapter 2, section 9). In this respect, the existence of customers within the area involving high as well as low network costs is of particular interest when determining whether the area is appropriate.[79]

240. Only persons and organizations that from a general point of view are qualified to operate the network may be granted a network concession (Chapter 2, section 10). The applicant's general competence, the structure of the organization and previous experience of network operation are factors that will be considered. In case of a concession for an area the applicant's qualifications are of particularly importance as the holder of such concession in principle will have an exclusive right to construct high-voltage lines within that area.[80]

III. Terms and Conditions and Validity Period

241. In general, a number of conditions are attached to a network concession. These conditions are determined by the Swedish Energy Agency in the individual concession, and shall include conditions for the construction works as well as the indisposition and use of installations, that are deemed necessary to ensure the security of the operations, the protection of human health and the environment from damage and inconvenience, the promotion of suitable long-term conservation of land, water and other resources, as well as any other conditions which for other reasons may be required from a public interest point of view (the Electricity Act, Chapter 2. section 11).

75. Electricity Act, Ch. 2, s. 10 and Prop. 1993/94:162, pp. 146–147.
76. Regarding the Planning and Building Act, *see generally* paras 607–610 *infra* .
77. In addition, the general provisions of the Environmental Code shall be applied in line with concession matters, namely the general rules of consideration in Ch. 2, the basic and special provisions for management of land and water in Chs 3–4 and certain provisions regarding environmental quality standards (Ch. 5, s. 3 and Ch. 16, s. 5); regarding these provisions, *see* paras 469–481.
78. Prop. 1996/97:136 pp. 44–45.
79. Prop. 1996/97:136 p. 124.
80. Prop. 1996/97:136 p. 125.

242. Network concessions are, as the main rule, granted for an indefinite period of time. (Chapter 2, sections 13–15a).

§3. Right to Use Land of Third Parties for Power Lines

243. A concession granted under the Electricity Act does not include the right to use for such purpose land owned by third parties. In order to construct a power line on the land of another party, the concession holder must either conclude some kind of right of user agreement with the landowner, or be granted a compulsory right (*tvångsrätt*) by application to the public authorities.

244. A compulsory right can be granted *inter alia* pursuant to the provisions of the Utility Easements Act (*Ledningsrättslagen, SFS 1973:1144*), which is the most common procedure, or by way of expropriation under the Expropriation Act (*Expropriationslagen* (*1972:719*).

245. If a concession has been granted for a power line, the concession holder has the right to be granted a utility easement based on the concession decision (Utility Easements Act, section 11).

246. For more details on the relevant land and cadastral legislation, including the Utility Easements Act and the Expropriation Act, *see* Part IV, Chapter 6 *infra*.

§4. Network Operations

I. Delimitation of Network Operations

247. A legal entity carrying out network operations, i.e., the holder of the network concession, is not allowed to engage in generation or trade in electricity (but may form part of group of companies that pursue the latter kinds of operations). Notwithstanding this restriction (legal unbundling), a legal entity conducting network operations may generate electricity if the generation is exclusively intended to compensate for losses in the network, or is performed by mobile reserve plants intended for occasional use during power outages (the Electricity Act, Chapter 3, section 1 a). The rationale of this rule is that the financial situation of the network operator will to some extent determine the size of the network tariff charged for the transmission of electricity through the network. Tariffs are subject to government regulations, whereas electricity generation and trade are not subject to similar restrictions. By separating operation and generation and trade into different legal entities, the network operation business will not be influenced by the commercial situation relating to the generation and trade business.[81]

248. In order to additionally ensure the independence of the network operator, the accounting and bookkeeping of network operations must be conducted and kept separately from any other activities (Electricity Act, Chapter 3, section 2). This rule also works to make it easier to determine whether the tariffs charged by the network

81. Prop. 1996/97:136 p. 136.

operator are objective and non-discriminatory. Moreover, all network operators, which are part of a group where generation or trade in electricity is carried out, must produce a supervisory plan that will ensure that such network operators act objectively and in a non-discriminatory manner (Electricity Act, Chapter 3, section 17).

249. The second and the third Electricity Markets Directives (2003/54/EC[82] and 2009/72/EC[83]) provide not only for the legal unbundling of network operations from other operations, but also for the *functional unbundling* of legal entities involved in network operations. In line with these Directives, the following applies to network operators that are part of a group whose combined network has at least 100,000 electricity consumers (Electricity Act, Chapter 3, section 1b–1e):

- Company organization and decision making must be separate from companies which pursue generation or trade in electricity.
- A member of the board, the managing director or authorized signatory of a company must not hold such a position in a company which pursues generation or trade in electricity.
- The company must not grant leading employees in a leading position salaries or other benefits which are based on the results of those parts of the group which pursue generation or trade in electricity.
- The company must also ensure that it can take independent decisions concerning the assets that it requires for operation, maintenance, reinforcement and expansion of the network.

250. The state-owned operator if the main transmission grid, *Svenska Kraftnät* (the Swedish TSO) is separated from operations involving generation and trade by way of its ownership structure.[84] Therefore, it fulfils the enhanced ownership unbundling requirements of the third Electricity Market Directive (*see* Electricity Act, Chapter 3, section 1f–1k).

II. Obligation to Connect Electrical Installations and to Transmit Electricity

251. Producers, traders and consumers of electricity must conclude an agreement with the holder of the network concession for the transmission of electricity. The holders of a network concession are obliged to connect an electrical installation to the power line or network on reasonable terms, unless there are special circumstances, for example, that there is an expected failure, lack of capacity or to pay of tariffs (the Electricity Act, Chapter 3, section 6).[85] Disputes relating to the conditions for the connection, including the tariffs charged by the concession holder are settled by the

82. This Directive was repealed by Directive 2009/72/EC.
83. Directive 2009/72/EC of the European Parliament and the Council of 13 Jul. 2009 concerning common rules for the internal market in electricity and repealing Directive 2003/54/EC.
84. The Energy Markets Inspectorate, Report EI R 2011:9, pp. 19–20.
85. Prop. 1996/97:136 p. 143.

Energy Market Inspectorate, whose decisions in such matters can be appealed to an Administrative Court of First Instance, *see* further paragraph 329 *infra*.

252. The fundamental TPA rule, stipulates that the holder of a network concession must allow the transmission of electricity through his power lines to any one person on reasonable terms (Chapter 3, section 9).

253. With respect to the national electricity grid, which is owned and operated by the state utility *Svenska Kraftnät*, the following applies. Large electricity producers and area networks may enter into an agreement with *Svenska Kraftnät* in order to connect themselves to the national grid. Most power links connecting to other countries are also owned by *Svenska Kraftnät*. Thus, in order to be able to carry out import or export of electricity, an agreement for transmission services must be concluded with *Svenska Kraftnät*. It should, however, be mentioned that no agreement with *Svenska Kraftnät* is needed for the cross-border transmission of power traded on the spot market of the Nordic power exchange, Nord Pool.[86]

254. As regards cross-border transmission of electricity, Regulation 714/2009[87] should be noted too. The Regulation, which entered into force on 3 March 2011, and is directly applicable in all Member States, aims at setting fair rules for cross-border exchanges in electricity. For this purpose, the Regulation *inter alia* contains provisions on a compensation mechanism between the TSO – i.e., in Sweden, *Svenska Kraftnät*– for cross-border flows of electricity and principles on harmonized principles on cross-border transmission charges and the allocation of available capacities of interconnections between national transmission systems in case of congestions.

255. In order to improve the management of the electricity transmission network and to allow trading and supplying electricity across borders in the Community, Regulation 714/2009 provides for the establishment of a European Network of Transmission System Operators for Electricity (the ENTSO for Electricity, the 'ENTSO-E'). The task of the ENTSO-E is *inter alia* to prepare network codes for cross-border transmission of electricity. The Swedish TSO for electricity, *Svenska Krafnät*, represents Sweden in the ENTSO-E network.

III. Regulation of Network Tariffs

256. For the connection of electrical installations to the network, the concession holder will charge a non-recurrent tariff. A tariff will also be charged for the transmission of electricity. Tariffs shall be based on objective and non-discriminatory grounds (the Electricity Act, Chapter 4, section 1).

257. Under the Electricity Act, tariffs for transmission of electricity shall be designed to ensure that the payment of the connection fee gives the customer free access to the entire electricity network in Sweden, except for connections with neighbouring countries (Chapter 4, section 2). Accordingly, a customer who is connected to the grid has access to the entire electricity market and can purchase electricity from

86. For general information regarding the Nord Pool power exchange, *see* paras 294–299.
87. Regulation (EC) No. 714/2009 of the European Parliament and of the Council of 13 Jul. 2009 on conditions for access to the network for cross-border exchanges in electricity and repealing Regulation (EC) No. 1228/2003.

any supplier based on the same network charge. This is an important principle for the functioning of an open electricity market.

In order to facilitate connection of renewable electricity production sources (typically wind power) and to mitigate so-called threshold effects, special provisions for the sharing of connection costs between different operators who benefit from the same capacity increase in the network may come into play according to new rules which apply as 1 May 2015 (Electricity Act, Chapter 4, section 9b). The 'threshold effect' means that the operator who is first to establish a renewable energy production source (e.g., a wind power plant) at a location where the network needs to be reinforced, must bear the entire cost of the investment, which may create an obstacle for investments in new wind power plants. Therefore, it has become possible for Svenska Kraftnät (the main grid operator) to finance the initial cost, which is then to be shared with other operators who establish themselves later. Thus, under the Ordinance (2015:213), network companies can apply for a grid reinforcement loan from Svenska Kraftnät. This has been described as an interim solution which is suggested to be followed by new regulations where the state does not bear any financial risk (*see* report Ei R 2015:08).

258. The tariffs (fees) of the network operators distributing electric power in Sweden have been subject to a regulation in arrears (*ex post*) until 2011. As of 2012, a new regulatory regime in advance (*ex ante*) has been introduced. The first regulatory model (for Distribution System Operator (DSO) and TSO) was based on the principle of cost-of-service (actual cost plus reasonable revenue) and has generally been described as a rather 'light-handed' regulation.

259. In 2005, the Swedish regulator implemented an incentive-based regulatory scheme for the distribution companies, the so-called Net Performance Assessment Model (NPAM). Under this model, actual revenues were compared with and benchmarked against the cost of constructing and operating a theoretical (virtual) network and a cost norm model. After several administrative court appeals, the NPAM was abandoned by the regulator in 2009. In the same year, the EU Court also held that the NPAM did not correctly implement the provisions of the second Electricity Market Directive (2003/54/EC)[88] and criticized the model's lack of legal certainty.[89] Thereafter, a 'transitory' regulatory *ex post* supervision model was applied until 2011 before the entry into force of the new regulation in advance in 2012.

260. From 1 January 2012, the regulator (the Energy Markets Inspectorate, the Ei) assesses the network companies' network fees in advance, in accordance with the new provisions of Chapter 5 of the Electricity Act and in line with the Electricity Market Directive (2009/72/EC). The new *ex ante* regulatory regime has focus on revenues. The regulator will decide in advance on the level of income (i.e., a revenue cap), which the companies are permitted to earn during the regulatory period. This length of period will be four years, unless special reasons apply (Electricity Act, Chapter 5, section 1 and section 4), meaning the first regulatory period set *ex ante* will be 2012–2015. For the main transmission network, the Government is entitled to decide

88. For a more detailed account of the net performance assessment model, *see* the 2005 edition of *Energy Law – Sweden*, para. 265.

89. Case C 274/08, *Commission v. Sweden*, judgment 29 Oct. 2009.

on other intervals, and has set the regulatory period for the TSO (*Svenska Kraftnät*) to one calendar year.

261. The network companies are obliged to apply for a revenue cap and submit to the regulator such information that is required to assess the application (Chapter 5, section 2). The decision on the revenue caps must be made by the regulator (Ei) at the latest two months before the regulatory period begins. In such decisions by the regulator, the data and methodology used in determining the revenue cap must be described (Chapter 5, sections 2–3). A decision applies directly and without prejudice to appeals – which can be made to an administrative court (Chapter 5, section 19).

262. The revenue cap must cover reasonable costs of operating the network during the period and provide a fair return on the capital invested. The quality of the manner in which the companies undertake their operations will also be taken into consideration (Chapter 5, sections 6–7).

263. The details of Sweden's regulatory model are decided by the regulator (Ei),[90] based on the framework legislation set out mainly in the Electricity Act and the Revenue Cap Ordinance (*SFS 2014:1063*). The applied regulatory model is structured on different cost items, where a division is made between Capital Cost (CAPEX) and Operating Cost (OPEX).

264. Regarding the capital cost, the assessment of the regulatory asset base is a very important part. The regulatory asset base is valued by the principle of replacement value with a method of linear depreciation over the asset's economic lifespan. To calculate the return on the regulatory asset base, the Swedish regulator uses the method of Weighted Average Cost of Capital (WACC).

265. The operating cost a divided in 'controllable cost' and 'uncontrollable cost' (e.g., costs relating to superior networks). The controllable cost, unlike the uncontrollable cost, is successively reduced by an efficiency target during the regulatory period.

266. The quality of transmission is set as a mean value for historic data on interruptions. At the end of the regulatory period, the actual quality outcome is compared with this historical value, and the rate of return on capital will be adjusted accordingly.

267. The structure of the Sweden's current regulatory model for electricity networks is shown below.

90. The Ei has issued a number of regulations for this purpose: on reporting (EIFS 2015:1), on calculation (EIFS 2015:2), on quality regulation (EIFS 2015:5) and on efficiency (EIFS 2015:6).

Figure 1, *Regulatory model*[91]

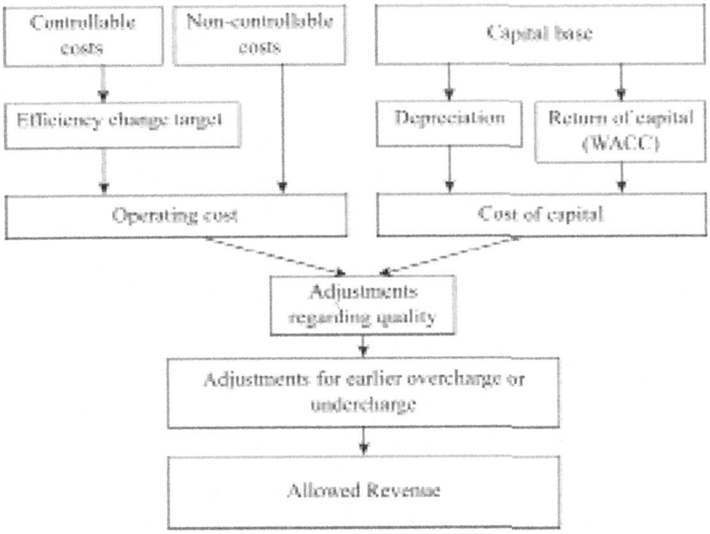

268. The revenue cap can, as the main rule, not be changed. However, certain exceptions apply. Upon request from the network company, the regulator can increase an individual revenue cap due to circumstances that are deemed to cause a significant increase of the revenue cap, or if special reasons apply. A request for a revised revenue cap can be made during the regulatory period or at the latest four months thereafter (Chapter 5, sections 10 and 12). In line with general principles of administrative law, the revenue cap shall be changed (i.e., reduced) by the regulator during the regulatory period if the network company has submitted incorrect or incomplete information, unless the impact on the revenue cap is minor. In addition, the revenue cap shall be changed (increased or decreased) by the regulator during the regulatory period if special reasons (e.g., the introduction of new EU-rules) apply (Chapter 5, section 11).

269. The regulator is obliged to reassess the revenue cap after the regulatory period, if it can be assumed that the cap is too high in view of actual circumstances that become known after the decision, unless the deviation is minor (Chapter 5, section 13). Any reassessment of the revenue cap by the regulator must be based on the same methodology that the regulator has used in its original decision (Chapter 5, section 14). To ensure equal treatment of operators, the Electricity Act prescribes that a network operator can apply for a reassessment of its revenue cap if an administrative court (following an appeal) has adjusted the revenue cap for another network operator and the same grounds for adjustment are applicable also for the applicant (Chapter 5, section 15).

270. At the end of the regulatory period, the network operator's actual revenue is compared with the revenue cap set by the regulator (including any adjustments, as described above). The deviations are carried forward to the next regulatory period,

91. NordReg, *Economic Regulation of Electricity Grids in Nordic Countries*, p. 28.

and will thus reduce (in case of 'overcharging') or increase (in case of 'undercharging') the revenue cap for the next regulatory period. If the actual revenue would exceed the cap by more than 5%, the network operator must pay an over-charging penalty (Chapter 5, sections 20–21).

The revenue caps for the first regulatory period 2012–2015 were subject to appeal court rulings of principal relevance *inter alia* with respect to the calculations of (elements of) the controllable costs and the regulatory calculus rent, *see cases* 61-14 et. al. (Kammarrätten i Jönköping). Also the revenue caps for the second regulatory period 2016–2019 are, at the time of writing, subject to legal proceedings concerning the level of the calculus rent in WACC-method.

§5. System Responsibility

271. By appointment of the Government, the state utility *Svenska Kraftnät* is the body which has the overall responsibility, the system responsibility, for the Swedish electricity system.[92] In this capacity, *Svenska Kraftnät* shall coordinate the operation of the electricity network (including connected installations) so that balance between the generation and consumption of electricity, both within the country as a whole and within parts thereof, is maintained in the short-term (cf. the Electricity Act, Chapter 8, section 1).

272. For the purpose of fulfilling its system responsibility, *Svenska Kraftnät* may order electricity generators to increase or decrease their power generation, against payment of a market-based compensation. If the balance of the system cannot be upheld by virtue of said measures, *Svenska Kraftnät* may order the holders of network concessions to limit or interrupt the supply of power to consumers. *Svenska Kraftnät* shall thereby, to the extent possible, consider the concession holder's undertakings with respect to security in supply (Chapter 8, section 2).

273. Svenska Kraftnät is responsible for controlling the overall balance of the electricity system, but it does not carry the final economic responsibility for this control. Instead, the economic responsibility in this respect rests with the entities that have assumed balancing responsibility for the terminal points (off-take points) in the system, *see* further paragraphs 282–289 *infra*. However, the balancing responsibility includes an economic relationship with *Svenska Kraftnät*. If the entity that has assumed balancing responsibility cannot supply the system with as much electricity as is taken out in the terminal points for which it is responsible, the difference will be supplied by *Svenska Kraftnät*. The entity responsible for balancing must then compensate *Svenska Kraftnät* for so-called balance power. Correspondingly, if the entity having the balancing responsibility has supplied the system with more electricity than it has taken out, then the entity will get paid by *Svenska Kraftnät* for the balance power.

92. In the sense of Directive 2009/72/EC, Svenska Kraftnät is the Transmission System Operator (TSO) for the Swedish transmission system (*see supra*).

§6. Obligation to Meter and Compute the Electricity Transmitted

274. The rules concerning metering of electric power are set out in the Electricity Act (Chapter 3, sections 10–14), the Ordinance on Metering, Calculation and Reporting of Transmission of Electric Power (*SFS 1999:716*) as well as in a regulation issued by the regulator, EI (*EIFS 2011:3*). Under the Electricity Act, the holder of the network concession is obliged to meter the quantity of electrical power transmitted, as well as its distribution over time. If the electricity consumer subscribes to a fuse not exceeding 63 Amperes, the holder of the network concession is required to make both a preliminary computation of the quantity of electrical power transmitted and its distribution over time, as well as a final metering of the electrical power transmitted and a computation of its distribution over time. This does not apply to an electricity consumer who has requested that the quantity of electrical power transmitted, as well as its distribution over time, be metered. Moreover, starting in 2012, all customers are entitled to hourly metering if they have concluded an electricity distribution agreement which contain terms which provide for hourly metering (Electricity Act, Chapter 3, section 10).

275. The network concession holder is obliged to report the results of the metering and the computations. Reports shall be furnished to the entities having the balance responsibility and to *Svenska Kraftnät*, amongst others. Detailed provisions regarding such reports are provided in the Ordinance regarding Reporting of Network Operations (*SFS 1995:1145*).

276. Costs for metering and the metering equipment, as well as the installation thereof, may be charged to the consumer only if the consumer has requested his power consumption to be metered in a manner other than set forth above. However, customers that have concluded an agreement which provide for hourly metering (*see infra*) cannot be charged any additional costs for such metering (Electricity Act, Chapter 3, section 11). The cost of the meter, including the equipment for the collection of metering data, as well as the installation thereof, at the input point from a power generator, shall be charged to the power generator by the network concession holder (Chapter 3, section 14).

Chapter 5. Supply and Trade

§1. General

277. As previously mentioned, as of 1 January 1996, supply of distribution and trade in electricity takes place on a free market with competition between the parties involved. Customers are free to choose whomever they want to purchase electricity from, including foreign electricity suppliers.

278. Unlike networks operations, no permits or concessions are needed for entities involved in supply of or trade in electricity. The Electricity Act only provides a limited set of rules with respect to said activities – namely provisions regarding balancing responsibility, and consumer protection, *see* paragraphs 282–289 and paragraphs 307–317 *infra.*

279. As mentioned in paragraph 247 *supra*, a legal entity carrying out network operations, i.e., the holder of a network concession, is not allowed to engage in trade in electricity (cf. Electricity Act, Chapter 3, section 1). Therefore, supply and trade will always take place through separate legal entities. However, except for the TSO (*see infra*), legal separation does not prevent a joint ownership, in as much that trading companies and network operators can belong to the same group of companies – they can, for example, have the same parent company.

§2. TPA to the Network

280. As described more in detail in paragraphs 251–255 *supra*, the fundamental principle of the deregulated electricity market is that suppliers, as well as buyers, are entitled to have electricity transmitted through the network. This right is expressed in the Electricity Act as an obligation for the network concession holder to transmit electrical power on behalf of others on reasonable terms (cf. Electricity Act, Chapter 3, section 9).

281. Moreover, the network concession holder is obliged to ensure the good quality of the transmission and to rectify deficiencies in the transmission, to the extent the rectification costs are reasonable in relation to the inconvenience suffered by the users as a result of the deficiencies.

§3. Balancing Responsibility and Notification Requirements

282. The Electricity Act provides that electricity suppliers are obliged to ensure that there is an entity who has assumed the 'balancing responsibility'(*balansansvar*) for the electricity consumer's terminal point, cf. Chapter 8, section 4. The balancing responsibility for a terminal point means the economic responsibility for the Swedish electricity system being supplied with as much electricity as is taken out at the terminal point in question. The terminal point is the off-take point at which an electricity consumer, in accordance with the agreement with the network concession holder, is supplied with electrical power for consumption, *see also* paragraphs 251–255 *supra*.

283. According to said provision of the Electricity Act, no delivery of electricity may take place before an entity having the balancing responsibility has been assigned for the relevant terminal point. The electricity trading entity can either assume the balancing responsibility itself or assign this task to another entity, which offers to undertake balancing responsibility as a service.

284. As described *supra*, the balancing responsibility also includes an economic relationship with *Svenska Kraftnät* with respect to so-called balance power. Hence, a company that wishes to assume balance responsibility must conclude an agreement with *Svenska Kraftnät* to this end.

285. foreign entity cannot assume balancing responsibility, unless it has a registered branch in Sweden. In order to be permitted to assume balancing responsibility, the entity has to demonstrate, *inter alia*, certain financial solidity. *Svenska Kraftnät* will assess the company's financial position in accordance with its credit policy. Depending on the outcome of such assessment, a financial security may be required.

286. The entity assuming balance responsibility is obliged to fulfil certain reporting requirements in relation to *Svenska Kraftnät inter alia* regarding generation and consumption forecasts. Detailed provisions on the reporting obligation are provided in the Ordinance regarding System Responsibility for Electricity (*SFS*: *1994:1806*).

287. Under the Electricity Act (Chapter 8, section 5), the electricity supplier supplying electricity to a consumer at a certain terminal point is obliged to continue to supply electricity until the consumer is no longer connected at the terminal point, or until another electricity supplier restarts to supply power to the consumer at the terminal point, or the transmission of electricity is permitted to be discontinued due to the consumer non-fulfilment of his duties towards the electricity supplier. The application of this supply obligation principle is important, as there is otherwise a risk that some consumers would be left without any electricity supplier. If that the situation would occur, there is no longer a party responsible for ensuring that there is an entity assuming balance responsibility at those consumers' terminal points. The economic responsibility for the consumer's consumption would then rest with *Svenska Kraftnät*.

288. A supplier of electricity, who has concluded a supply contract with a customer, must notify the holder of the network concession that it will deliver electricity in the customer's feed-in point. The notification must also contain information on the entity which has assumed the balancing responsibility at the off-take point. Deliveries can at the earliest start fourteen days after the submission of such a notification (Electricity Act, Chapter 8, sections 6–7).

289. Furthermore, a supplier of electricity must continuously notify the regulator of the prices and delivery terms that the supplier applies in relation to the users (consumers) of electricity (Electricity Act, Chapter 8, section 11 b). The supplier must also inform its customers of the origin of the electricity supplied and the CO_2 emissions which the generation of such electricity has caused (Electricity Act, Chapter 8, section 12). Detailed provisions on these notification and information requirements are set out in regulations issued by the Ei.[93]

---

93. EIFS 2010:2 and EIFS 2011:4.

§4. Export and Import

I. Direct Trade

290. As a consequence of the deregulations of the electricity markets in the Nordic countries in the mid-1990s, entities acting on the market in one of these countries have access to the electricity networks of the other countries, and consumers have a free choice of electricity supplier in any of these countries. By virtue of the market deregulations on the EU level, the same conditions in principle applies (or will apply) vis-à-vis other Member States.

291. The Electricity Act provides a possibility for the Swedish State to exercise certain control over trade in electricity with other countries, in the sense that network concessions for links to other countries are granted by the Government, *see* paragraph 237 *supra*.

292. Prior to 2003, agreements involving import or export of electric power for a period of six months or more had to be notified to *Svenska Kraftnät*. The purpose of this former information requirement was to enable market evaluations, for example with respect to reliability of the supply and price development on the Swedish market.[94] This requirement was repealed in 2003,[95] as it was considered being of no practical use, due to *inter alia* the small number of long-term export and import contracts.[96]

293. A foreign electricity supplier may not assume the so-called balancing responsibility for a Swedish electricity customer's terminal point, *see* paragraphs 282–289 *infra*. Thus, if a consumer is buying electricity directly from a foreign supplier, the consumer has to assume balancing responsibility itself or enter into an agreement with a Swedish entity assuming the balancing responsibility for the consumer's off-take point.

II. Trade on the Nord Pool Power Exchange

294. Norway was the first of the Nordic countries to deregulate its power trade. The new Norwegian Energy Act, of 1990, formed the basis for the deregulation in the other Nordic countries. Established in 1993, the Nordic Power Exchange (Nord Pool), was the world's first multinational exchange for trading electric power. Today, Nord Pool is also the world's largest market of its kind, and provides the leading market for buying and selling power in the Nordic region, as well as Estonia, Lithuania, Germany and Great Britain.[97]

295. Nord Pool is a market place for trading in power contracts for physical delivery and in financial power contracts (futures, forwards, etc.). Another business area is clearing of bilateral power contracts.

---

94. Prop. 1993/94:162 pp. 165–166.
95. *SFS 2002:121*.
96. Prop. 2001/02:56 p. 36.
97. *See* http://www.nasdaqomx.com/commodities.

296. In Nord Pool's auction-based spot market for trade in power contracts for physical delivery (Elspot), hourly power contracts are traded for physical delivery next day (day ahead market). Nord Pool Spot AS is owned by the Nordic TSOs Statnett SF, Svenska Kraftnät, Fingrid Oyj, Energinet.dk and the Baltic TSOs Elering and Litgrid. Nord Pool Spot AS is licensed by the Norwegian Water Resources and Energy Directorate (NVE) to organize and operate a market place for trading power, and by the Norwegian Ministry of Petroleum and Energy to facilitate the power market with foreign countries.

297. Elbas is Nord Pool's physical market for power trading in hourly contracts for delivery today and tomorrow (intra-day market). Continuous adjustment trading in hourly contracts can be performed up until one hour before the delivery hour. The participants are mainly power producers, distributors, industries and brokers in Finland and Sweden.

298. On Nord Pool's financial market, traders can hedge the price of electricity by means of futures and forwards. Thus, the traders may use financial contracts to secure the prices of buying and selling power for a period of up to four years. Electricity certificates and emission allowances under the EU ETS (*see supra*) are also traded.

299. The price on the Elspot market serves as a reference for the price of the forwards on the financial market as well as the remainder of the electricity market. Thus, the formation of prices for the entire Nordic electricity market takes place on the Nord Pool power exchange.

§5. REMIT

300. In October 2011, the European Parliament and the European Council adopted Regulation (EU) No. 1227/2011, Regulation on Wholesale Energy Market Integrity and Transparency (REMIT). As an EU regulation, REMIT is now directly applicable in all Member States.

In simplified terms, REMIT has four main elements:

- Prohibition of insider trading (Article 3) and of market manipulation (Article 5).
- Obligation of market participants to register with their competent National Regulatory Authorities (Article 9).
- Obligation of market participants to report wholesale energy market transactions (Article 8) and to publish insider information (Article 4).
- Authorization of ACER (the European Agency for the Cooperation of Energy Regulators) to monitor the market (Article 7), to collect transaction reports (Article 8) and to register market participants (Article 9).

REMIT has a wide scope and defines a 'market participant' as any legal or natural person carrying out transactions in wholesale energy products. The definition encompasses energy traders, TSOs, regulated exchanges for electricity or gas markets and energy brokers.

Further. REMIT defines 'wholesale energy products' as physical and financial contracts for electricity or for natural gas where delivery is in the EU. The definition includes the supply and transportation contracts as well as derivative transactions, such as options or swaps. However, supply and distribution contracts to consumers and industrial clients consuming less than 600 GWh per year are excluded from the regulation.

Under REMIT, the enforcement and sanctioning of possible violations of the regulation is the responsibility for the Member States. Consequently, the competencies of national regulatory authorities (in Sweden: the Energy Markets Inspectorate) and the nature of sanctions are a question for national law. Accordingly, the Act on Measures against Market Abuse in Wholesale Energy Trading (SFS 2013:385)[98] has been adopted for these purposes.

98. Lag (2013:385) om ingripande mot marknadsmissbruk vid handel med grossistenergiprodukter.

Chapter 6. Consumption

§1. General

301. In 2011, electricity use in Sweden amounted to 129.2 TWh. From 1970 until 2005, the consumption of electricity increased by an average of 3% annually, but this continuous increase has now been broken. The use of electricity is linked mainly to two sectors, the residential and service sector, and the industrial sector, whereas electricity use in the transport sector is relatively small.

302. As described in paragraphs 247–250 *supra*, entities engaging in trade in electricity and in transmission of electricity (network operations) must conduct said activities through separate legal entities. As a consequence, the consumer, apart from entering into an agreement with an electricity supplier of its choice, must also conclude an agreement with an entity transmitting electricity, i.e., the holder of the network concession in the relevant area or for the relevant line.

303. On the deregulated Swedish electricity market, the consumer's cost for electrical power can be said to consist of the following components:

- the price for the electricity (the 'commodity price');
- the price for the transmission of electricity on the network, *see* paragraphs 256–270 *supra* regarding network tariffs;
- the cost of the electricity certificates and emission allowances, *see* paragraphs 212–222;
- taxes such as energy tax and Value Added Tax (VAT), *see* Part V, Chapters 2, 3 and 4 *infra*.

304. The price for the electricity (the commodity price) makes up approximately 40% of the total electricity cost. By changing supplier, the consumer has some possibility to affect the price of the electricity. The network tariff accounts for about 20% of the cost, while taxes and VAT account for the remaining 40%.

305. The Swedish Competition Authority (*Konkurrensverket*) supervises that effective competition on the electricity market is maintained. The interaction between the electricity legislation and the competition legislation will be further described in Part VI *infra*.

306. The remainder of this chapter shall be devoted to the special household customer protection provisions that are entailed in the Electricity Act.

§2. Consumer Protection with Respect to Transmission and Supply of Electricity

307. Chapter 10, sections 9–16 of the Electricity Act contains mandatory provisions on compensation for interruptions (outages) in the transmission of electricity to end users of electricity. Such compensation must as the main rule be paid by the grid owner (concession holder) if the transmission of electricity is interrupted for more than twelve hours. This kind of compensation has the form of liquated damages, whose size depends on the length of the interruption. The maximum amount of liquidated damages payable for each interruption period corresponds to 300% of the end user's estimated annual network charge. Liquidated damages for interruptions pursuant to the said rules will be deducted from other kinds of damages that an end user could be entitled to due to interruptions.

308. Chapter 11 of the Electricity Act contains certain mandatory rules of protection relating to transmission and supply of electrical power to consumers. The Electricity Act defines a *consumer* as a physical person to whom electricity is transmitter or supplied mainly for purposes other than industry, business or trade – i.e., household customers (Chapter 11, section 2). Contractual terms which are to the disadvantage of the consumer compared to the provisions of Chapter 11 will be deemed not valid.

309. The consumer must enter into agreements regarding supply and transmission of electricity in order to ensure its consumption. Normally, these agreements are in a standardized format with very limited possibilities for the consumer to negotiate more favourable terms and conditions. The Consumer Sales Act (*Konsumentköplagen, SFS 1990:932*), which provides mandatory consumer protection rules relating to purchase of personal property, is not applicable to purchase of electricity or transmission of electricity.[99] Given this background and the opinion that the consumer protection level on the electricity market should be similar to other areas, the legislator has deemed it necessary to include certain mandatory minimum rules in the Electricity Act.

310. Transmission of electricity to a consumer may be interrupted only if the consumer neglects his obligations and the neglect constitutes a substantial breach of contract. If the circumstances give reasons to believe that the interruption may result in injury to person or damage to property which is not insignificant, the electricity supply must not be interrupted. However, this will not apply in the event the consumer acts improperly (the Electricity Act, Chapter 11, section 3). Before the supply is interrupted, the consumer shall be given a possibility to rectify the default within a reasonable time and be informed that the supply may otherwise be interrupted.

311. If the default consists of the consumer's failure to pay in due time the costs for the transmission or the supply of electricity, the transmitting entity may send a notice with a payment request to the consumer along with a notification that the supply will be interrupted unless the consumer pays the outstanding amount within three weeks after receipt of the request. Such notification regarding non-payment shall at the same time be sent to the social welfare board in the municipality where the electrical power is transmitted (Chapter 11, section 4).

312. If the consumer pays his debt, or disputes the payment claim, the supply may not be interrupted. Nor may the supply be interrupted should the welfare board announce to the entity submitting the notification that it agrees to assume the responsibility for payment of the debt.

313. Notwithstanding the restrictions relating to interruptions described above, the network concession holder may interrupt the supply of electrical power for the

99. As opposed to the sale of electricity, the Consumer Sales Act is deemed applicable with respect to the sale of natural gas to household customers; *see* Part II *infra* .

purpose of ensuring the electricity safety or to maintain the required level of operational and supply security (Chapter 11, section 7).

314. Should the consumer's rights with respect of rectification and notification not be observed before interruption of the supply, the consumer is entitled to damages from the network concession holder for the damage incurred, or in the event the transmission was interrupted upon instruction from the supplier of electricity, from the supplier (Chapter 11, section 8).

315. In the event that the transmission of electricity to a consumer is interrupted because of an obstacle within the control of the network concession holder, the consumer is, as the main rule, entitled to compensation for the damage and loss that he suffers as a result of the interruption (Chapter 11, section 10). If the interruption is not caused by an act or omission of the consumer (or by any of the other reasons set forth *supra*), the consumer is entitled to damages from the network concession holder, provided that the latter cannot show that the interruption is caused by an (i) obstacle, which is (ii) beyond his control, and which he (iii) could not reasonably have taken into account, and (iv) the consequences of which he could not reasonably have avoided or overcome (Chapter 11, section 10). For example, extreme weather conditions for the geographical area in question, as well as other exceptional events, will, in general, fall outside the network concession holder's 'control sphere' and meet the other prerequisites for exclusion of liability.[100]

316. The damages to which the consumer may be entitled under Chapter 11 include expenses, loss of income and other losses resulting from the interruption. When determining the amount of damages, the consumer's insurance cover, his possibility to obtain insurance cover and to predict and avoid the damage, as well as other relevant circumstances, shall be considered (Chapter 11, section 11).

317. In addition, supply contracts with consumers must contain certain mandatory information, and the supplier must notify the consumer on price increases and changed contractual terms. The supplier must also provide information on consumer rights and the handling of complaints or disputes. The change of supplier must always be free of charge for a consumer (Chapter 11, sections 13–20).

100. Prop. 1996/97:136, ss 192–193. *See also* ARN (the National Board for Consumer Complaints) decisions of 20 Dec. 2002 (Case no. 2002-1286) and 24 Feb. 2003 (Case no. 2002-5265), where ARN considered that extreme weather conditions were at hand and ruled against the consumer's request for compensation.

Chapter 7. Supervision and Penal Provisions

§1. Authorities

318. Supervision of the compliance with the Electricity Act, as well as ordinances and regulations issued on the basis of that Act, is exercised mainly by the following three authorities, appointed by the Government.

319. The Energy Markets Inspectorate (the Ei) is the main supervisory authority under the Electricity Act. The Ei supervises, amongst other things, compliance with respect to connection and access to the electricity networks, including connection charges and network tariffs. It combines the roles of regulator, licensing authority and supervising authority for the electricity natural gas and district heating markets.

320. *Svenska Kraftnät* is the state utility assigned with overall system responsibility for the Swedish electricity system, and supervises conformance as to the operational security of the national power system.

321. The Swedish National Electrical Safety Board handles and supervises technical safety issues.

§2. The Right to Issue Instructions and Orders

322. The supervisory authorities are generally empowered to issue requests for the documents and information as may be required for the purpose of the supervision. Such requests may be combined with a penalty (Electricity Act, Chapter 12, section 2).

323. Moreover, the supervisory authorities may issue instructions and orders necessary in order to ensure compliance with the relevant rules. Such instructions or orders may be combined with penalties.

324. As regards security issues relating to the operations of the national power system and electricity safety issues, the relevant supervisory authority may:

order a rectification at the expense of the party concerned, should the latter not comply with an order issued under Chapter 12, section 3 for the purpose of electricity safety;
- prohibit the use of an electrical installation where the state or use thereof may pose a threat to human life or property;
- prohibit the supply or use of electrical equipment where the state or use thereof may pose a threat to human life or property, or which has not been duly controlled, tested, inspected or documented in accordance with the applicable regulations; and
- prohibit the supply of services that may pose a threat to human life or property due to defective or incorrect installations of electrical equipment.

325. Also, the above-mentioned measures may be combined with penalties (Chapter 12, section 4). For the purpose of supervising the electricity safety or the security relating to operations of the national power system, the relevant supervising authority may gain access to all relevant areas, sites and facilities and test all devices intended for connection to electrical installations, or electrical equipment introduced to, or due to be introduced to, the market.

§3. Fines for Delay

326. In the event the network operator fails to submit in due time a duly certified copy of its annual report, together with an auditor's certificate required under the Ordinance (*SFS 1995:1145*) regarding auditing of network operations, the network operator is liable to pay a fine amounting to SEK 10,000–SEK 20,000. Additional fines will be added to such amount until the network operator actually delivers the required reports (Chapter 12, sections 7–8).

§4. Penal Provisions

327. The Electricity Act contains certain penal provisions (Chapter 13). A fine or a sentence of a maximum of one year's imprisonment is imposed on those who:

- construct or use electrical power lines or connects transformer stations or substations for which line concessions are required, without having obtained a network concession;
- ignore, neglect or violate the terms and conditions issued in relation to the network concession; or
- ignore, neglect or violate instructions issued for the purpose of the safety operation of the national power system, as well as other instructions regarding electrical equipment, devices and installations.

328. Further, fines are imposed on those who by negligence or by intent disconnect, during a period longer than three years, a line covered by a line concession, without the prior consent of the Government. In minor cases, however, no liability will be imposed.

§5. Appeals

329. Decisions by the supervisory authorities under the Electricity Act may, as a main rule, be appealed to an Administrative Court of First Instance, and from there to an Administrative Court of Appeal (subject to the grant of a review permit) (Chapter 13, section 5).

Part II. Regulatory Framework Concerning Natural Gas

Chapter 1. Introduction

330. Sweden uses relatively small quantities of energy gases in comparison with many other European countries, and natural gas accounts for only a small portion of the Swedish energy supply. Currently, the Swedish natural gas network mainly covers the west coast area, including the cities of Malmö and Gothenburg, whereas the Stockholm capital region as well as eastern and northern parts of the country is not connected to the network. It is only around 30 out of the 290 municipalities in Sweden that have access to natural gas. In 2014, natural gas represented approximately 2% of the country's total energy supply. However, in regions covered by the natural gas network, natural gas provides about 20% of the energy use.[101]

331. The end users on the Swedish natural gas market has decreased during the recent years; however, there has been an increased demand and rising volumes. In 2010, a record volume, 1.6 billion cubic metre (18.7 TWh) was consumed in Sweden, however during 2014 the volume was down to approximately 10.2 TWh mainly due to warm weather.[102] In principle, all natural gas consumed in Sweden is currently imported from Denmark through one single pipeline. The gas deliveries from Denmark are foreseen to be reduced on a longer term perspective due to reduced volumes from Danish gas fields.

332. The Swedish natural gas market is deregulated. As from 2007, the gas market in Sweden, as in most EU countries, is totally open to competition – meaning that natural gas customers are entitled to freely choose their gas supplier in accordance with the provisions of the Gas Market Directive (2009/73/EC).[103]

333. This Part II deals mainly with the sector specific regulatory legislation governing the construction of natural gas pipelines and the transmission and storage of natural gas. Other legislation which has bearing on the Swedish natural gas sector – primarily environmental law, tax law and competition law – will be addressed separately in Parts IV, V and VI, respectively.

101. Energy Markets Inspectorate, EI R2015:16, The Swedish electricity and natural gas markets 2014, p. 42.

102. *Ibid.*, p. 42.

103. Directive 2009/73/EC of the European Parliament and of the Council of 13 Jul. 2009 concerning common rules for the internal market in natural gas and repealing Directive 2003/55/EC.

Chapter 2. Legal Framework

§1. EU Legislation

334. The legal framework for natural gas in Sweden is to a considerable extent based on EU legislation. The Swedish legislation, primarily the Natural Gas Act (*see infra*), implements the so-called EU's third energy package, including the Gas Market Directive 2009/73/EC.[104] This third legislative package for natural gas aims at increasing transparency and competition on the market.

335. The first Gas Market Directive (98/30/EC) abolished national supply monopolies in the various Member States and opened up for competition on the gas markets in the EU. The Gas Market Directive (2003/55/EC),[105] which repealed Directive 98/30/EC, had the aim of opening the internal gas market for all customers and required *inter alia* a legal unbundling of network activities from supply of natural gas and the establishment of a common minimum set of responsibilities for national regulatory authorities.

336. Directive 2009/73/EC is intended to harmonize the legislative framework and promote the development of cross-border trade in order to create efficient and competitive markets for gas. The Directive provides provisions regarding further unbundling between network operators and suppliers of natural gas and strengthened consumer rights.

337. Increased responsibilities and strengthened roles for the regulatory authorities are provided by the establishment of the Agency for the Cooperation of Energy Regulators (ACER) and enhanced cooperation between the regulatory authorities by the new union organization ENTSO-G (European Network of Transmission System Operators for Gas). The Gas Market Directive also contains provisions regarding binding rules (Network Codes) to be drawn up by ENTSO-G and non-binding rules (Framework Guidelines) to be developed by ACER.

338. Other relevant EU legislation include Regulation no. 715/2009 regarding conditions for access to the natural gas transmission networks, which establishes harmonized standards and rules for network access and TPA services, congestion management, transparency, balancing and the trading of capacity right.

---

104. The acts related to natural gas are Directive 2009/73/EC of the European Parliament and of the Council of 13 Jul. 2009 concerning common rules for the internal market in natural gas and repealing Directive 2003/55/EC, Regulation (EC) No. 715/2009 of the European Parliament and of the Council of 13 Jul. 2009 on conditions for access to the natural gas transmission networks and repealing Regulation (EC) No. 1775/2005, and Regulation (EC) No. 713/2009 of the European Parliament and of the Council of 13 Jul. 2009 establishing an Agency for the Cooperation of Energy Regulators. Sweden declared in September 2012 that the Third Energy Package Directives have been fully implemented.

105. Directive 2003/55/EC of the European Parliament and of the Council of 26 Jun. 2003 concerning common rules for the internal market in natural gas and repealing Directive 98/30/EC.

339. Furthermore, Regulation (EU) No. 994/2010 concerning security of natural gas supply[106] establishes rules aimed at safeguarding the security of gas supply by ensuring the proper and continuous functioning of the internal market in natural gas, by allowing for exceptional measures to be implemented when the market can no longer deliver the required gas supplies. The Regulation also provides for the definition and allocation of responsibilities among natural gas undertakings, Member States and the EU as regards both preventive actions and reactions in case of disruptions of supply.

§2. National Legislation

340. On the national level, the following statutes form the main legislative framework with respect to Sweden's natural gas law:

- The Natural Gas Act (*Naturgaslag, SFS 2005:403*).
- The Act on Certification of Certain Natural Gas Companies (*Lagen om certifiering av visa naturgasföretag, SFS 2011:711*).
- The Ordinance on Revenue Caps in the Natural Gas Area (*Förordning om fastställande av intäktsram på naturgasområdet, SFS 2014:35*)
- The Environmental Code (*Miljöbalken, SFS 1998:808*).
- The Minerals Act (*Minerallag, SFS 1991:45*).
- The Act on Security of Gas Supply (*Lagen om trygg naturgasförsörjning, 2012:273*).

341. The provisions of the Natural Gas Act lays down the general principles of regulatory system in the natural gas sector with respect to the construction of pipelines and transmission of natural gas. The Natural Gas Act is supplemented by ordinances issued by the Government and regulations issued by the regulatory authority in the natural gas sector; the Swedish Energy Markets Inspectorate.[107]

342. Before the adoption of the Natural Gas Act,[108] regulatory issues regarding natural gas pipelines were primarily dealt with in the Pipelines Act (*Lag om vissa rörledningar, SFS 1978:160*), which dates from 1978. Prior to the adoption of the Natural Gas Act, the Pipelines Act contained concession rules for the construction of natural gas pipelines and provisions enabling TPA for transmission of natural gas under specified circumstances. The Pipelines Act is still in force with respect to certain other kinds of pipelines – for example, those used for the transmission of crude oil and

106. Regulation (EU) No. 994/2010 of the European Parliament and of the Council.
of 20 Oct. 2010 concerning measures to safeguard security of gas supply and repealing Council Directive 2004/67/EC.

107. The Government has issued three Ordinances under the Natural Gas Act: the Natural Gas Ordinance (2006:1043), the Ordinance (2006:1051) on accounting and auditing of the transmission of natural gas, and operation of degasification plant, the Ordinance (2000:672) on natural gas charge, and the Ordinance (2014:35) on Revenue Caps in the Natural Gas Area (Förordning om fastställande av intäktsram på naturgasområdet.

108. The first Natural Gas Act (SFS 2000:599) came into force 1 Aug. 2000.

district heating – but explicitly exclude natural gas pipelines from its current scope of application.[109]

343. The Act on Certification of Certain Natural Gas Companies implements the rules in Directive 2009/73/EC regarding certification of TSOs. The Act on Security of Gas Supply implements the Regulation (EU) No. 994/2010 concerning security of natural gas supply.

344. The Environmental Code is the main Swedish environmental statute. The provisions of the Code have *inter alia* to be observed in connection with the construction and operation of natural gas pipelines. The Environmental Code, as well as other relevant environmental legislation, is described more in detail in Part IV *infra*. However, certain aspects of the environmental legislation will also be addressed in this Part II.

345. The Minerals Act regulates the right to explore and exploit mineral resources, including oil and natural gas. Since Sweden has no indigenous oil or natural gas reserves, the provisions of the Minerals Act have no practical relevance as far as natural gas is concerned. A general description of the Minerals Act is given in Part IV, Chapter 3, *infra*.

109. Pipelines Act, s. 1, para. 1.

Chapter 3. Natural Gas Production and Exploitation

346. The natural gas consumption in Sweden amounts to approximately 10–12 TWh annually. Sweden has no indigenous production of gas and is therefore 100% import dependent on gas supplies from Denmark. The supply line via Denmark ends in Sweden, and thus there is no transit of natural gas through Sweden.

347. The Danish natural gas resources are foreseen to be emptied in a relatively near future, causing a challenge for the future supply of natural gas to Sweden. Since Sweden has no possibility to extract natural gas of its own and is dependent upon gas import via a single supply point, there are a number of projects for production and transmission of biogas in the natural gas system in progress. Domestically produced biogas is increasing in Sweden but the produced volume of biogas is not sufficient to compensate for a future decrease of Danish natural gas. Between 1% and 2% of the natural gas distributed in Sweden is biogas.[110] Biogas requires enrichment of propane before it can be inserted in the natural gas network in order for the biogas to comply with the quality of the natural gas. The distribution system operator is responsible to ensure that the injected biogas complies with the imported natural gas.

348. During the 1970s and 1980s, a number of exploration projects with regard to oil and natural gas were carried out in Sweden, both onshore and offshore. None of these projects have led to any exploitable findings, except for a minor oil well on the island of Gotland in the Baltic Sea.

349. According to the Minerals Act (*Minerallag, SFS 1991:45*), which is applicable for exploration and exploitation of a number of mineral substances, including gaseous hydrocarbons and oil on land and within private water areas in the sea, a special licence is required. The exploration of the seabed and subsoil in public waters area as well as outside the territorial waters in the Swedish economic zone, for the purpose of exploiting natural resources, is subject to the provisions of the Continental Shelf Act (*Lag om kontinentalsockeln, SFS 1966:314*), and (in the economic zone), the Act on Sweden's Economic Zone (*Lag om Sveriges ekonomiska zon, SFS 1992:1149*).

350. Further to the Minerals Acts, the Continental Shelf Act and the Act on Sweden's Economic Zone, *see* Part IV, Chapter 3 *infra*.

110. EI R2012:11, The Swedish Electricity and Natural gas Markets 2011, p. 60.

Chapter 4. The Natural Gas System

§1. Transmission Network

351. All natural gas, which is imported to Sweden, is currently transported through the Danish transmission network, which is owned and operated by Energinet.dk – a Danish state-owned company that has the role as TSO with system responsibility for the Danish natural gas system.[111]

352. The Swedish natural gas network consists of transmission, distribution grid and storage. Transmission means transport of natural gas through a network, which mainly contains high-pressure pipelines, with the exception for high-pressure pipelines that are primarily used for local distribution of gas (Chapter 1, section 6a). The Swedish transmission grid extends from Dragör, south of Copenhagen in Denmark, via Malmö in the south, to Gothenburg to Stenungsund in Sweden, with a branch pipeline to Gislaved and Gnosjö in the province of Småland. A number of minor branch lines adjoins the main pipeline and connects towns in the southern and western part of the country to the network. The total length of the high-pressure transmission grid, including branch lines, is 620 kilometres.

353. The owner of the transmission network is Swedegas AB, which is also the TSO. Between 2010 and 2015, Swedegas was owned by the venture capital company EQT and was acquired in 2015 by Spanish Enágas and Belgian Fluxys.

354. Alternative gas network connections to the Swedish grid have been projected over the years. A project for a pipeline between Germany, Denmark and Sweden – the Baltic Gas Interconnector – was planned for the connection of the existing gas networks of southern Scandinavia and other European countries, and permits from the governments of the three countries were given during 2004–2006. The project has however not been implemented yet.

355. In 2009, the Swedish government granted Nord Stream AG a permit to build a 1,224 kilometre long natural gas pipelines from Vyborg, Russia to Lubmin, Germany, through the Swedish economic zone in the Baltic sea. The construction of the two pipelines was completed during 2012. At the time of writing (March 2016), there are no plans of connecting the Nord Stream to the Swedish natural gas grid.

§2. Distribution Network

356. Distribution of natural gas, which means transport of natural gas through local pipelines to consumers, is performed in Sweden via approximately 2,700 kilometres of distribution lines, owned by different gas distribution network companies.[112]

357. There are six DSO in Sweden, the largest being E.ON Gas Sverige AB in terms of the length of the pipelines and the number of connection points for outtake

111. www.energinet.dk.

112. Energy Markets Inspectorate, Ei R 2015:i6, p. 35.

of natural gas. Other operators of distribution networks are the municipal (or semi-municipal) energy companies Göteborgs Energi Gasnät AB, Kraftringen Nät AB, Öresundskraft AB, Varberg Energi AB and Stockholm Gas AB.

Stockholm Gas AB owns the gas network for household use and vehicle gas in the Stockholm region, with a total pipeline length for household gas of approximately 500 kilometres and for vehicle gas approximately 40 kilometres. In April 2014, Swedish Parliament decided that the Stockholm network would be covered by the regulations under the Natural Gas Act and that Stockholm Gas AB would be regulated in the same manner as other Swedish network companies and also assume balancing responsibility.[113]

§3. Liquefied Natural Gas

358. Liquefied Natural Gas (LNG) is imported to Sweden, mainly from LNG production plants in Norway. The first LNG terminal in Sweden came into operation in 2011 and is located in Nynäshamn, south of Stockholm. LNG is transported to the plant via ships. The terminal in Nynäshamn is not connected to the gas transmission network in the south-western part of Sweden. Thus, the gas from the terminal is transported to the gas networks by tankers or lorries. In 2014, a new terminal was opened in Lysekil, and other LNG import terminals are being planned in other coastal cities in Sweden, e.g., Gothenburg, Helsingborg and Gävle.

§4. Storage

359. Natural gas can either be stored in special storage facilities or in the transmission pipelines by way of compression (the so-called line-pack).

360. Sweden has no storage for equalization of consumption over seasons, but only a small facility for consumption peaks. This storage facility (lined rock cavern), called Skallen, is located in the province of Halland and is owned and operated by Swedegas. It has a maximum capacity of approximately 10 million cubic metre at 200 bar and the daily withdrawal capacity varies from 0.6 to 0.9 million cubic metre, which corresponds to 10%–20% of the gas demand in Sweden during wintertime. The variation depends on the pressure prevailing in the storage facility and the pipelines.[114] For seasonal storage, Sweden must rely on facilities outside of the country or line-pack flexibility in the national grid.[115]

113. Government bill 2013/14:74.
114. IEA, Oil & Gas Security 2012, Sweden, p. 17.
115. Energy Markets Inspectorate, *The Swedish Electricity and Natural Gas Market* 2014, p. 48.

Chapter 5. Network Operations

§1. Concession Requirements

361. Under Chapter 2 of the Natural Gas Act, the construction and operation of natural gas pipelines and storage facilities are subject to a concession (licence) system, which is summarized *infra*.

362. Concessions are granted by the Government after examination by the regulatory authority, the Swedish Energy Markets Inspectorate. The main conditions for the granting of a concession to construct and operate a natural gas pipeline, or a storage facility, are the following:

- The natural gas facility must be suitable from a public point of view. The purpose of the suitability assessment is mainly to prevent the construction of facilities that are socio-economically unnecessary – i.e., that pipelines are not constructed in areas where the transmission, distribution or storage capacity is already sufficient so that pipeline-to-pipeline competition is avoided – or pipelines being run in such a manner that they cause unnecessary intrusion to the detriment of third parties.
- The applicant for a concession should be suitable from a public point of view to pursue the operations covered by the concession.
- The concession must not be in conflict with a detailed development plan or regional regulations under the Planning and Building Act (*see generally* paragraphs 607–610 *infra*). However, minor deviations can be allowed, unless they are contrary to the purpose of the development plan or the regional regulations.
- Certain provisions of the Environmental Code (*see generally* Part IV, Chapter 2 *infra*) shall be applied in the concession matter, and an EIA pursuant to the Environmental Code must be included in an application for a concession. Furthermore (as regards pipelines), the concession shall relate to a natural gas pipeline having, in principle, a predetermined extension.
- A concession is normally subject to certain conditions, usually for the protection of general public interests and individual rights, such as security, health and environmental issues. A concession can be conditioned upon the providing of security for costs related to a removal of a pipeline or a facility and restoration.

363. A concession, as the principal rule, shall be granted for a period of forty years. Upon application by the concession holder, the duration of the concession can be extended by forty years at each time.

364. A concession for a natural gas pipeline or storage facility must not be transferred to another natural or legal person without the permission of the Swedish Energy Markets Inspectorate. The suitability of the transferee shall be examined in the same manner as in the case of an application for a new concession.

365. A concession may be revoked if the natural gas pipeline is no longer used and is not needed to safeguard the supply of energy, or if the concession holder would fail to meet his obligations.

366. If a concession should expire, the last holder of the concession is responsible for removing the natural gas pipeline and adopting other restoration measures if this is necessary from the public or individual viewpoint.

367. Concession is not required where, for example, a pipeline that is located after (downstream) a metering and regulation station (MR-station) – i.e., low-pressure pipelines which are used mainly for distribution of natural gas to individual companies or households.

§2. Legislation for the Laying of Pipelines

368. A concession granted under the Natural Gas Act does not include the right to use land owned by third parties. In order to construct a natural gas pipeline on the land of another party, the concession holder must either conclude some kind of right of user agreement with the landowner, or be granted a compulsory right (*tvångsrätt*) with respect to the land in question.

369. A compulsory right may be granted *inter alia* pursuant to the provisions of the Utility Easements Act (*Ledningsrättslagen, SFS 1973:1144*), which is the most common procedure, or by way of expropriation under the Expropriation Act (*Expropriationslagen, SFS 1972:719*).

370. If a concession has been granted for a natural gas pipeline, the concession holder has, as a matter of principle, the right to be granted a utility easement in accordance with the concession decision (Utility Easements Act, section 11).

371. For more details on the relevant land and cadastral legislation, including the Utility Easements Act and the Expropriation Act, *see* Part IV, Chapter 6 *infra*.

372. The laying of a natural gas pipe lines in water areas is subject to a special permit requirement for water operations under the Environmental Code (*see generally* paragraphs 492–499 *infra*). If a concession has been granted for the pipeline, a permit for water operations shall as the main rule be granted.

373. In addition, a pipeline that extends outside the Swedish territorial waters limit on the continental shelf must be separately approved by the Government pursuant to the Continental Shelf Act, *see* paragraphs 599–601 *infra*.[116]

374. Finally, certain other legislation must also be observed, *inter alia* the Planning and Building Act, as well as in certain cases, the Road Act and the Act concerning Cultural Heritage Management – regarding these Acts, *see* paragraphs 607–618 *infra*.

§3. Obligations of Owners of Natural Gas Pipelines

375. An undertaking that owns a natural gas pipeline and is involved in transport of natural gas is responsible for the operation and maintenance and, where applicable,

116. Continental Shelf Act, s. 15 a.

the development of the grid or interconnection to other systems. The undertaking is also responsible for ensuring that the system is safe, reliable and efficient, and the long-term ability to meet reasonable requirements for the transport of gas.

I. TPA and Connection to the Natural Gas Network

376. In accordance with the requirements in Regulation 715/2009/EC,[117] the access to the Swedish gas transmission network is fully open for third parties and transparent. Under the Natural Gas Act, the owner of a natural gas pipeline is obliged to provide connection and access to the network for the transport of natural gas on behalf of a customer or a natural gas undertaking on reasonable terms (Chapter 3, sections 5–6). This obligation to connect or transport gas does not apply where a pipeline does not have sufficient capacity or if there are other special grounds.

377. An owner of a natural gas pipeline is obliged to transport natural gas on reasonable terms. However, none of the obligations regarding access and transport apply where the pipeline is used solely by the owner. As regards connections charges and tariffs for transport of natural gas, *see* further paragraphs 387–394 *infra*).

II. Legal and Functional Unbundling

378. The Gas Market Directive (2009/73/EC as well as the previous 2003/55/EC) contains detailed unbundling provisions, in particular Articles 9 and 26 of the Directive 2009/73/EC. The unbundling rules entail separation of legal entities conducting operations involving the transmission and distribution of natural gas from entities trading or producing natural gas. The Natural Gas Act has implemented these rules in such a way that an undertaking involved in transport of natural gas is not allowed to conduct trade in natural gas. A TSO is also not allowed to be involved in production of natural gas or production of or trade in electricity, and shall be independent of undertakings involved in production of or trade in natural gas or electricity (Chapter 3, section 2–2a).

379. A person that independently or together with another exercises control over an undertaking conducting production of or trade in natural gas or electricity may not exercise any right or control towards a TSO, and vice versa. Persons that are able to appoint members of the supervisory board or similar organs of a TSO are not entitled to exercise any right or control towards an undertaking conducting production of or trade in natural gas (Chapter 3, section 2b).

380. The same person is barred from being a member of the supervisory board, a managing director, an authorized signatory or another person with a similar position of both an undertaking involved in production of or trade in natural gas and a TSO. Further, the unbundling rules entail provisions as regards the obligation for an operator to ensure that commercially sensitive information or staff of such operator is transferred

117. Regulation (EC) No. 715/2009 of the European Parliament and of the Council of 13 Jul. 2009. On conditions for access to the natural gas transmission networks and repealing Regulation (EC) No. 1775/2005.

to other undertakings or other parts of the operator undertaking (Chapter 3, section 2c–e).

III. Accounting and Auditing

381. In order to ensure non-discriminatory access to the network and avoid cross-subsidizing – i.e., that a financial surplus from the network operations (the natural monopoly) is used for subsidizing operations that are open to competition – it is necessary to separate the network business from those activities of a vertically integrated natural gas undertaking which compete on the market, namely production and supply. According to Directive 2009/73/EC (Article 31), there shall be an unbundling of accounts of natural gas undertakings, which in their internal accounting, shall keep separate accounts for their natural gas transmission, distribution, LNG and storage activities. Revenue from ownership of the transmission or distribution network shall be accounted separately.

382. The provisions on accounting unbundling in Directive 2009/73/EC are incorporated in the Natural Gas Act (Chapter 3, section 3). The accounting provisions of the Natural Gas Act are supplemented by detailed regulations issued by the Swedish Energy Agency.[118] Further, under the Act, the auditor of a natural gas undertaking that pursues the transmission of natural gas or the storage of natural gas on behalf of third parties shall undertake a separate examination of the accounts for these operations (Chapter 3, section 4).

§4. Obligations for Owners of Storage and Gasification Facilities

383. The Natural Gas Act contains similar obligations for owners of storage and gasification facilities as is stated for owners of natural gas pipelines. The owner of a storage facility is obliged to store natural gas on behalf of a third party on reasonable terms. Equally, an owner of a gasification plant shall grant TPA on reasonable terms (Chapter 4, sections 5–6).

384. As regards unbundling, rules on legal and functional separation principally provide that an owner of a storage or gasification facility is not entitled to conduct trade in natural gas. The same person may not act as a board member, managing director or authorized signatory for both an undertaking involved in storage or gasification and an undertaking conducting trade (Chapter 4, section 2). Accounts and audit shall also be kept separate from other operations carried out by the undertaking.

118. STEMFS 2006:3 – Regulations and general advice on accounting and auditing of operations concerning transmission of natural gas, storage of natural gas and operation of degasification plant.

§5. System Responsibility

385. According to the Gas Market Directive, Member States shall approve and designate undertakings which own transmission, storage or LNG facilities as system operators for these facilities. The obligation for a TSO is to carry out the function of transmission and to be responsible for operating, maintenance and development of the transmission system and its interconnections with other systems, and for ensuring the long-term ability of the system to meet gas transmission demands. TSOs shall be certified by the national regulatory authorities (Article 10).

386. According to the Swedish Natural Gas Act, system responsibility means the responsibility to ensure that the short-term balance of the natural gas system as a whole is maintained, i.e., that the aggregated off-take of natural gas equals the aggregated input of gas to the system (Chapter 7, section 1).

In August 2012, Swedegas was certified by the Ei as TSO for the Swedish gas market, and in May 2013, the balancing responsibility was assigned from *Svenska Kraftnät* to Swedegas.

§6. Network Tariffs

I. Connection Charges

387. The Natural Gas Act provides that the charges and other conditions for connection to a natural gas pipeline shall be reasonable, objective and non-discriminatory. When setting the charges, consideration shall particularly be given to the location of the pipeline or the plant that shall be connected, and the capacity of the connection point (Chapter 6, section 1).

II. Tariffs for Transport, Storage and Gasification

388. Tariffs for transport and storage of natural gas and for access to a gasification facility shall be reasonable, objective and non-discriminatory. Consideration shall, for the setting of tariffs, *inter alia* be taken to the number of connected customers, geographical location of the customers, transported volumes and the capacity (Chapter 6, sections 2–3).

389. The Ei shall, prior to the application of a charge or other condition, audit and approve the methods used for establishing the connection charges and other conditions. Such approval is granted if the methods are presumed to ensure objective and non-discriminatory charges. If the Ei does not approve the methods, the authority shall decide upon the methods that are to be applied by the network owner (Chapter 6, section 5).

390. Under the Natural Gas Act, tariffs for transport, storage and gasification shall be published, and the undertaking is obliged to provide written information regarding the tariff on request (Chapter 6, section 4).

III. Regulation of Network Tariffs

391. From 1 January 2015, the regulator (the Energy Markets Inspectorate) assesses the gas network companies' fees for transmission and distribution of natural gas to their customers. The provisions for the regulation of network tariffs are set out in Chapter 6 of the Natural Gas Act, and are in conformity with Article 41.6 of Directive 2009/73/EC, which provides that the regulatory authorities shall be responsible for fixing or approving sufficiently in advance at least the methodologies used to calculate or establish the terms and conditions for connection and access to national networks, tariffs and access to LNG facilities.

392. The regulation of network tariffs for natural gas is a so-called *ex ante* regulation, which corresponds to the *ex ante* regulation for electricity, *see* paragraphs 256–270 *supra*. The advance review includes the natural gas undertakings' revenues from connection, transport and storage as well as access to gasification facilities. A revenue cap is established prior to a certain period of four years, the first regulatory period being 2015–2018. A revenue cap shall be decided separately for transmission, distribution, storage and operation of gasification plants (Chapter 6, section 6).

393. The network companies shall apply for a revenue cap and submit to the regulator of the information required to assess the application (Chapter 6, section 7). The regulator shall issue its decision on the revenue caps at the latest two months prior to a new regulatory period. The decision shall include a description of the data and methodology used for the determination of the revenue cap (Chapter 6, section 8). The regulator's decision on a revenue cap is directly applicable but can be appealed to an administrative court (Chapter 6, section 23).

394. The revenue caps shall cover reasonable costs for the operation of the network and provide a reasonable capital yield on the capital invested (Chapter 6, section 10). The capital return is calculated according to the method of weighted average cost of capital (WACC). The regulatory asset base, on which the return is calculated, shall be decided according to the Ordinance on the Determination of Revenue Cap for the Natural Gas Sector (SFS 2014:35) and detailed regulations decided by the regulator (*see* in particular EIFS 2014:6 concerning reasonable costs and rate of return in natural gas operations). The Natural Gas Act constitutes the framework legislation while the regulator has a relatively wide scope to decide upon the details in the regulatory model for revenue frames.

395. As a main rule, the revenue cap cannot be changed during the regulatory period but some exceptions apply. After the regulatory period, the revenue cap may be reassessed, for instance if the regulator deem that the cap has been too high in relation to actual circumstances during the regulatory period or if the company applies for an increase of the revenue frame (Chapter 6, sections 15–16).

396. At the end of the regulatory period, the actual income of the network operator shall be compared with the revenue frame set by the regulator. In case of deviations, such deviating amounts will be carried forward to the following regulatory period and will reduce or increase the next revenue cap. If a natural gas company has over-charged with more than 5% during the regulatory period, a penalty must be paid by the company (Chapter 6, sections 19–20).

Chapter 6. Wholesale and Supply

§1. Market Actors

397. As Sweden does not produce natural gas of its own, all supply of natural gas is transported from Denmark. The Swedish market is therefore closely linked to the Danish gas market and the market exchange Gaspoint Nordic. Trade on Gaspoint Nordic is concluded by physical delivery and all trading participants, shippers, must have a shipper agreement with the Danish TSO, Energinet.dk.

There is no wholesale market hub in Sweden as all gas is imported.

398. With respect to distribution to end customers (retail market), there are currently eight natural gas suppliers (gas traders) active on the Swedish natural gas market. The largest participants on the market are E.ON Gashandel Sverige AB, Dong Energy AB and Göteborgs Energi AB.

399. A gas supplier purchases natural gas from a gas producer or another gas supplier/trader within or outside Sweden and sells it to gas users in competition with other gas suppliers on the market. In Sweden, there is a free right of establishment for gas suppliers, meaning that an undertaking willing to act as a gas supplier on the market is not subject to any eligibility assessment or public records.[119] The total number of customers' switches of supplier is low, equivalent to about 0.15% for companies and 1.3% for domestic customers.[120]

§2. Balancing Responsibility

400. Balancing responsibility refers to the economical responsibility which shall ensure that the off-take of natural gas at every consumer's off-take point equals the volumes of gas transmitted into the grid (Chapter 7, section 4).

401. Short-term imbalances in the Swedish natural gas system are in the first place managed through market mechanisms, and second, where commercial solutions are insufficient, by physical restrictions in supply.

402. According to the Natural Gas Act, there should be an entity charged with balancing responsibility at every natural gas consumer's off-take point. This responsibility generally rests with the gas supplier. However, a gas supplier may commission another party to be balancing responsible. The undertaking having the balancing responsibility shall enter into a balance agreement with the TSO.

119. SOU 2010:30, p. 313.
120. Energy Markets Inspectorate, Ei R2015:16, p. 44.

Chapter 7. Consumption

§1. Gas Consumption and End Customers

403. Natural gas was introduced in Sweden in 1985, when the transmission pipeline from Denmark was taken into operation. The number of end users has decreased during recent years, but there is nevertheless a tendency towards increasing sold volumes of natural gas. A reason for this trend could be the increased use of LNG and production of biogas.

404. About 2% of Sweden's total energy supply constitutes of natural gas, but in regions covered by the natural gas network (mainly the western parts of the country) natural gas provides about 20% of the energy use. There are about 41,000 natural gas consumers, of which approximately 34,000 are domestic customers and the remaining are companies or industrial customers. In 2014, the total natural gas consumption amounted to approximately 10 TWh, and during recent years, the consumption has been declining.[121]

405. Sweden is currently increasing its biogas production and domestically produced biogas is transported in the natural gas system. In 2014, the biogas production totalled approximately 1.8 TWh. Around half of this production was used for vehicles and one-fourth was consumed in heat plants.

406. The largest group of end customers of natural gas in Sweden are industry customers, on the one hand, and cogeneration (CHP) and district heating plants on the other. Industry consumes 38% of the gas, and the CHP and district heating plants 25%. Household consumers (approximately 34,000) account for about 2%. The remaining amount is used in other businesses.[122] The number of customers on the Swedish natural gas market has decreased in later years.

§2. Consumer Protection

407. The Gas Market Directive has introduced a number of strengthened consumer protection provisions into the Natural Gas Act. These provisions are mandatory and are, among other things, specifically aimed at protecting consumers (vulnerable customers) from unreasonable or immediate interruptions of the supply of natural gas.

408. For the protection of the consumer, transmission of natural gas may only be interrupted if the consumer neglects his obligations and this negligence can be considered a significant breach of contract. Before supply is interrupted, the consumer shall be requested to rectify the breach. Where negligence involves failure to pay, the consumer shall be notified that supply may be interrupted if payment is not made within three weeks. The Social Welfare Board shall also be notified of the situation.

121. Statistics from the Swedish Energy Agency.

122. Statistics from the Swedish Energy Agency.

If the consumer rectifies the breach, or if the Social Welfare Board accepts responsibility for settling the debt, the distribution may not be interrupted (Chapter 8, sections 3–4).

409. Natural gas distribution may not be interrupted when a debt is subject to dispute. Nor may it be interrupted if there is reason to believe that interruption would entail personal injury, which is not of an insignificant nature, or extensive property damage, unless the consumer has been guilty of 'improper actions' (*agerat otillbörligt*). If the pipeline owner or the supplier of natural gas should interrupt the transmission or supply of gas to a consumer contrary to the provisions of the New Natural Gas Act, they can be liable to pay damages to the consumer (Chapter 8, section 8).

410. Furthermore, the Natural Gas Act stipulate detailed provisions of required information in a contract for transmission to a consumer, *inter alia* where pricing information can be obtained, conditions for invoicing and payment, contract term and termination conditions (Chapter 8, sections 13–14). A supplier or a company involved in transmission must inform consumers of their rights and on their web pages provide information on where to hand in complaints and relevant authorities for dispute solution, etc. A consumer is entitled to change supplier without charge and shall be notified of the possibility of changing supplier. Suppliers or owners of pipelines hall also have stipulated routines for handling of complaints (Chapter 8, sections 18–20).

411. In addition to the natural gas legislation, the Swedish consumer protection legislation contains certain provisions which are applicable to the supply of natural gas to individuals in their capacity of consumers (i.e., household customers). These provisions are found in three acts: the Consumer Sales Act (*Konsumentköplagen, SFS 1990:932*), the Act on Contractual Conditions in Consumers Relations (*Lag om avtalsvillkor i konsumentförhållanden, SFS 1994:1512*) and the Domestic Sales and Distance Sales Consumer Protection Act (*Distans- och hemförsäljningslag, SFS 2005:59*).

412. Since the general consumer protection legislation in some instances is difficult to apply with respect to the special circumstances which apply to the sale of natural gas, the Consumer Sales Act provides that the provisions of the Act shall not apply to the sale of pipeline supplied natural gas to consumers, provided that the general terms and conditions that govern the sale and purchase of such gas have been approved in advance by the Swedish Consumer Protection Authority (*Konsumentverket*). Therefore, standard agreements which have been approved in this special manner is commonly used for the sale to Swedish household customers.

Chapter 8. Supervision

413. The Ei is the Swedish regulator and the supervisory authority appointed by the Government in accordance with the Natural Gas Act. In this capacity, the Ei shall supervise the conformance to the Natural Gas Act and the regulations or conditions issued on the basis of the Act, as well as the Natural Gas Directive. The Ei may issue the directives or injunctions necessary to ensure such conformance. It also has the right to request information and gain access to the documents needed for the supervision. Failure to comply with a directive or to an information request by the Ei may be made punishable by fines under the Natural Gas Act (Chapter 10).

414. Supervision decisions made by the Ei having legal or factual effects for individuals or entities, can, as a principal rule, be appealed to an Administrative Court of First Instance (*förvaltningsrätt*), and from there further in the hierarchy of administrative courts (Chapter 11, section 4).

415. The supervision by the Ei is financed by a special fee, which is payable by operators of transmission pipelines and distribution pipelines in proportion to the annual volume of natural gas transmitted through the pipelines. This fee is SEK 0.0005 per delivered kWh gas lower heating value.[123]

123. Natural Gas Act, Ch. 10, s. 5, Ordinance (2008:1330) on Natural Gas Fee.

Part III. Regulatory Framework Concerning Oil, Coal and District Heating

Chapter 1. Oil and Coal

§1. The Oil Market[124]

416. In 2010, the total energy supply in Sweden was 614 TWh, whereof approximately 31% came from crude oil and oil products. Compared to 1970 where crude oil and oil products generated 350 TWh, Sweden is less dependent on the oil supply today. This is mainly a result of fuel oil and gas oil gradually having been replaced by electricity and district heating. Since 1988, however, the oil share of the total energy production has been quite constant, varying by less than 2% units from the mean value.

417. Sweden has no indigenous production of oil, but a significant refinement industry. The majority of the crude oil imported to Sweden is re-exported after refinement. In 2011, the net import of crude oil amounted to approximately 19,000 million tonnes. Oil was imported mainly from Russia (approximately 50%) and Norway, Denmark and the United Kingdom, i.e., from the oil fields in the North Sea. The transport sector accounts for the major part of the total oil consumption in the country.

§2. The Coal Market

418. Up to and including the 1950s, imported coal was of great importance to Sweden's energy supply. However, coal was gradually replaced by oil, which was cheaper and easier to handle. Due to the oil crisis in the 1970s, with the substantial rises in the oil price, coal once again became an attractive energy source because of its price and availability. During the 1990s, stricter environmental standards for coal burning as well as increased taxation of heat production in particular have led to lower use of coal.[125]

419. Today, coal and coke is mainly used by the industry and to a minor extent in combined heat and power stations and heating plants. Swedish industry uses steam

124. Swedish Energy Agency, *Energiläget 2012*.
125. Swedish Energy Agency, *Energiläget 2003*, p. 25.

coal, metallurgic coal and coke, and smaller volumes of other coal products like graphite and pitch. In 2010, the energy supply from coal and coke was 26 TWh, corresponding to approximately 4.2% of total energy supply (614 TWh).

§3. Legal Framework Concerning Oil and Coal

I. General

420. The regulatory framework with respect to oil, coal and coke can be summarized as follows.

421. The Environmental Code contains a number of general and specific provisions which apply with respect to *inter alia* the handling and storage of oil, coal and coke. The Code is also applicable with respect to the operations of, for example, condensing power plants and CHP-facilities, where oil, coal and coke are used as fuel, and plants where coal and coke are manufactured and oil refined (*see generally* paragraphs 486–491).

422. The *Combustibles and Explosives Act* (*see* paragraphs 611–615) also contains provisions applicable to the handling of oil and oil products.

423. As regards import, sale and trade in oil, the special obligations to maintain contingency stocks, as well as connected reporting requirements, have to be observed (*see* paragraphs 425–430 *infra*).

424. The tax legislation includes a complex set of energy and environmental taxes, such as taxes levied on emission on CO_2 and sulphur, which are relevant to suppliers and consumers of oil and oil products and coal.

II. Obligation to Maintain Minimum Stocks of Oil

425. As mentioned *supra*, the total supply of crude oil and oil products contributes to about 30% of the total supply of energy in Sweden. Although, the dependence of oil has decreased since the 1970s, the country is still dependent on international supply. In order to secure the supply of oil and coal during war and peace-time oil and coal crises, certain strategic storage is prescribed pursuant to the Act on Contingency Storage of Coal and Oil (*Lag om beredskapslagring av kol och olja, SFS 1984:1049*). This Act has been repealed as of 30 December 2012, but will continue to apply until 31 March 2013 with respect to contingency storage that began in 2012 (*see infra*). In order to implement the provisions of Directive 2009/119/EC,[126] new legislation applies as from 30 December 2012, namely the Act on Contingency Storage of Oil (*lag om beredskapslagring av olja, SFS 2012:806*), as supplemented by the Ordinance on Contingency Storage of Oil (2012:873).

426. The Directive 2009/119/EC imposes obligations on Member States to maintain minimum stocks of crude oil and/or petroleum products. These obligations

126. Council Directive 2009/119/EC of 14 Sep. 2009 imposing an obligation on Member States to maintain minimum stocks of crude oil and/or petroleum products.

are partly linked to an international agreement on a common energy programme under the framework of the International Energy Agency (IEA) – the IEA agreement.

427. According to section 2 of the Act on the Contingency Storage of Oil, Sweden must ensure that it maintains oil stocks corresponding to at least ninety days of average daily net imports or sixty-one days of average daily inland consumption, whichever of the two quantities is greater. The storage obligation concerns crude oil and certain other petroleum fuels (storage fuels), as defined in EU Regulation no. 1099/2008.

428. Under the Act on Contingency Storage of Oil, the obligation to keep a contingency storage of fuel oil concerns anyone who: (i) has imported crude oil or storage fuels to Sweden and also has sold or consumed storage fuels within the country, or (ii) has purchased storage fuels from an entity being subject to a storage obligation, and has sold at least 50,000 cubic metre storage fuels in the country (Chapter 3, section 1). By decision of the Government, the storage obligation may also apply with respect to local authorities.

429. The Swedish Energy Agency decides who is required to store oil and the sizes of the individual stores, based on sales or consumption quantities during the reference year (being the calendar year before the storage year). Each storage year runs from 1 April to 31 March of the following year.

430. The Swedish Energy Agency monitors compliance with the storage obligations under the Act on Contingency Storage of Oil. Those who do not meet their obligations are required to pay a daily fee, which is determined based on the capital cost of the product plus a penalty of, at the highest, 1,000% of the capital cost. Furthermore, the Act provides that a party failing to submit reports and other required information will be liable to pay a fee of currently SEK 10,000–SEK 25,000. Penalties and fees can be reduced or set aside only if extraordinary circumstances apply (Act on Contingency Storage, Chapter 8, sections 7–8).

III. The Sulphur Ordinance

431. The Sulphur Ordinance (*Svavelförordningen, SFS 2014*) is applicable to fuels containing sulphur. The Act contains limit values regarding emissions from the burning of fuel oil or other sulphur fuels, from use of sulphur fuel in industrial plants and energy production plants. The County Administrative Board is entitled to grant individual exemptions from the limit values.

The sulphur Ordinance also contains limit values for maritime fuels. The limit values can be higher if the ship is equipped with an exhaust cleaning system defined in the Ordinance.

432. The Ordinance generally prohibits sale, transfer or usage of burning oil or diesel burning oil to be used as fuel, if the sulphur content exceeds certain weight percentages.

433. A seller of sulphurous fuel shall inform the buyer of the sulphur content in the fuel in question when the sales agreement is entered into, unless it is obvious that the sulphur content is below the limit values. Moreover, anyone who sells, or imports for his own account, sulphurous fuel shall within three months from the sale or the import to Sweden inform the County Administrative Board hereof, provided that – due to the sulphur concentration in the fuel – the burning of the fuel without the use of purification measures is not permitted based on the limit values set forth in the Ordinance.

Chapter 2. District Heating

§1. General Background[127]

434. In technical terms, district heating can be described as the centralized production and supply of hot water, distributed through a pipeline system and used for the space heating of buildings, primarily in urban areas. District heating is produced in hot water boiler plants, which supply only heat, or in cogeneration plants (CHP-facilities), which supply both heat and electricity.

435. The district heating systems in Sweden were substantially expanded during the period from 1975 to 1985, not least due to their ability to replace oil through its flexibility of fuel use, and the expansion has continued since then, although at a more modest rate.

§2. Market Structure

436. Sweden has a vast net of distribution pipelines for district heating. District heating is most competitive in urban areas of high building density, and the system is well developed in larger cities and towns all over the country.

437. In 2014, the total energy supply to the district heating sector was approximately 54 TWh, corresponding to approximately 10% of the total energy supply of 555 TWh. The fuel mix in district heating plants has changed considerably over the last twenty years. In 1980, over 90% of the fuel input for district heating and CHP plants was in the form of oil. Today, the fuel mix is more varied, with bio fuels and waste being the main energy sources (67%). The change to other energy sources can be partly explained by the CO_2 tax, which has worked to reduce the use of fossil fuels.[128]

438. The environment in many Swedish urban areas has been significantly improved as a result of the expansion of district heating, which has reduced emissions of Sulphur Dioxide (SO_2), NO_x, particulates and soot. Energy policy has favoured district heating through various forms of state support, e.g., grants for the extension of existing district heating systems and the connection of group heating systems and even of individual buildings.[129]

439. Until the beginning of the 1980s, most district heating systems were owned and operated as services provided by the local authorities. During the 1990s, most of them were restructured into limited liability companies owned by the municipalities. Following the deregulation of the electricity market in the mid-1990s, there has been a considerable consolidation of ownership as a result of the larger electricity utilities acquiring local municipal energy companies, including their district heating operations.

127. The facts and figures under this section is mainly collected from the Swedish Energy Agency, *Energiläget 2014*, 41–45.

128. The Swedish Energy Agency, *Energiläget 2012*, pp. 58.

129. The Swedish Energy Agency, *Energy in Sweden 2003*, p. 21.

Nevertheless, over 50% of the country's district heating facilities are still owned by municipalities, or co-owned between private and public parties. In total, there are over 200 companies supplying heat in Sweden. However, the fact that production sources and the district heating networks often have the same owner, as well as difficulties for third parties to gain access to the networks, tend to limit competition on the district heating market. Unlike electricity and natural gas, the district heating market has not been deregulated, and customers cannot freely choose their heat supplier.

§3. Legal Framework for District Heating

440. The main legal framework for district heating is contained in the District Heating Act (*fjärrvärmelag, SFS 2008:263*). This Act contains a rather mild regulatory framework, which in brief can be summarized as follows.

441. The suppliers of heat – which in general also operate the distribution network – are obliged to submit price information to the regulatory authority, the Energy Markets Inspectorate. The customer is entitled to request negotiations regarding the price and other terms for the supply of district heating, or concerning the costs for a connection. Both parties may refer the matter to mediation, which is handled by a special public authority, the District Heating Board (sections 19–26). The Board can issue such injunctions that are required for the mediation, but is not a decision-making regulator in the same manner as the regulator under the Electricity Act and the Natural Gas Act (*see supra*). The District Heating Act also contains certain rules concerning termination of supply which aim to protect of household customers (sections 27–36).

442. Due to reform of the District Heating Act in 2014, a regulated TPA regime has been introduced, however in a less stringent form than in the electricity and natural gas areas. Hence, district heating companies are obliged to negotiate with third parties requesting access to the network. (section 37). If an agreement cannot be reached, the third party can request a regulated access on reasonable terms to the district heating network according the provisions of sections 37 a – 37 d of the District Heating Act. However, the owner of the network is not obliged to connect a third party if the owner can show that there is a risk that it will suffer damage due to the connection. Also, certain other exceptions from the TPA-obligations exist. Connection disputes are assessed by the regulator, the Energy Markets Inspectorate (Ei).

443. District heating undertakings who distribute (sell) district heating are obliged to account and report for these activities separately (sections 40–43). With respect to municipal companies, certain special rules apply to enable fair competition with private undertakings. Therefore, municipal companies are obliged to operate on 'commercial grounds', meaning that the municipal principle of 'self-cost' does not apply in this respect. Moreover, municipal undertakings are allowed to operate networks outside the boundaries of its home municipality, provided that such operations are conducted in the vicinity of the municipality and that they serve the purpose of achieving proper operation conditions (sections 38–39).

Part IV. Interaction between Energy Law and Environmental Law

Chapter 1. Introduction

444. Almost all generation, conversion and use of energy give rise to some form of environmental impact. The perhaps most significant effects on the environment are those related to emissions from the combustion of different kinds of fossil fuels. Such effects include *inter alia* the increase of concentration of GHG in the atmosphere, the precipitation of acidifying substances, and other forms of pollution of air, water and land.

445. Other environmental impacts are related to the location and construction of facilities for generation or transmission of energy. Even production forms which are not related to the combustion of fossils fuels or other fuels, such as hydropower or wind power, can have significant impact on the environment in the form of their effects to the nature and the landscape. Such environmental impacts also arise in connection with the exploitation or winning of different of minerals, or other natural resources, used to produce energy.

446. In addition, several energy processes give rise to waste products, e.g., ashes from the combustion of fossil fuels or spent nuclear fuel from nuclear power plants. Hence, waste management is an important issue in this context too.

447. The goal of Sweden's energy policy is, both on short and long term, to safeguard the supply of electricity and other energy on competitive terms. The energy policy shall create conditions for efficient and sustainable use of energy and a cost-efficient energy supply, with minimum adverse effects on health, the environment and climate, whilst at the same time supporting the transformation to an ecologically sustainable society.

448. In 2010, the Swedish Parliament adopted a national environmental objectives system, which consists of goals on three levels – a generation goal, environmental quality objectives and milestone targets.[130] The *generational goal* is the overall goal defining the changes and basic conditions required in the society for solving environmental problems within one generation and in order for the environmental quality objectives to be met.

449. Sixteen *environmental quality objectives* have been stipulated by the Parliament,[131] which describe the state of the Swedish environment. They define the

130. Prop. 2009/10:155.

131. Cf. SOU 2009:83 and Prop. 2004/05:150 and 2009/10:155.

necessary characteristics (qualities) of the natural environment and the cultural heritage environment in order to ensure environmentally sustainable development in Sweden. Sweden's environmental work is based on these sixteen environmental quality objectives, which are aimed to be achieved within one generation (i.e., by year 2020).The environmental objectives are used at the local and regional levels, in land use planning and decision-making. The Swedish Environmental Protection Agency (*Naturvårdsverket*) is responsible for the coordination and follow-up of the environmental objectives.[132]

450. The *milestone targets* are decided by the Government and are steps to be taken in order to achieve the generational goal and the environmental quality objectives.

451. Apart from the national objectives, the cooperation on the transnational level is becoming increasingly important. The development of the environmental laws of Sweden, and of other Member States, is largely driven by the development of EU environmental law. The Swedish energy policy is also based on the same three pillars as the energy cooperation within EU – ecological sustainability, competition and secured supply. The principle of sustainable development is enshrined as one of EUs fundamental aims, and a high degree of environmental protection and a better environment are prioritized.[133]

452. Furthermore, measures at the international level have significant impacts on Swedish environmental law. Sweden is a party to approximately forty international environmental conventions and agreements, such as, for example, the Espoo Convention, which contains rules on EIAs in a transboundary context, and the Kyoto Protocol which provides for measures and commitments to reduce greenhouse emissions.[134]

453. This Part IV deals with the interaction between energy law and environmental law based on the points of departure referred to above. Chapter 2 begins with a brief survey of the Swedish Environmental Code, which is the fundamental instrument of Swedish environmental law, where particular emphasis will be devoted to energy-related regulations as indicated above. Several other environmental statutes, not included in the Environmental Code, are of relevance in the energy sector too. The most important of those statutes will be addressed *infra* (Chapters 3–4). Furthermore, Sweden's undertakings with respect to climate policies and emissions trading will be dealt with in Chapter 5. Finally, a brief overview on certain aspects of Swedish land and cadastral legislation will be provided.

---

132. Examples of environmental quality standards are Reduced Climate Impact, Clean Air, A Non-toxic Environment, Good-quality Ground Water and Sustainable Forests. Cf. the webpage of the Swedish Environmental Protection Agency, http://www.naturvardsverket.se.

133. Treaty on EU, Art. 3.

134. An overview of the more important of these environmental conventions and agreements is given on the Internet home page of the Swedish Environmental Protection Agency, http://www.naturvardsverket.se.

Chapter 2. The Environmental Code

§1. Introductory Overview and Scope of Application

454. The Environmental Code (*Miljöbalk, SFS 1998:808*) entered into force on 1 January 1999. Before this date, Swedish environmental legislation consisted of a large number of different acts. Thus, one purpose of the Code was to compile the bulk (but not all) of Swedish environmental legislation in one instrument of legislation. Even though most of the provisions of the Environmental Code existed prior to 1 January 1999, a considerable amount of the rules came into force through the Code.

455. The overall aim of the Environmental Code (Chapter 1, section 1) is to promote a sustainable development that ensures present and future generations a healthy and sound environment. To this end, the Code is to be applied so that:

- human health and the environment will be protected against damage and nuisance, regardless of whether this is caused by pollution or other influences;
- valuable natural and cultural environment will be protected and conserved;
- biological diversity will be preserved;
- the use of land, water and the physical environment in general is such as to secure long-term good management in ecological, social, cultural and economic terms; and
- reuse and recycling, as well as energy conservation and other management of material, is promoted so that an eco-cycle is created.

456. The sixteen environmental quality objectives decided by Parliament (*see supra*) are not legally binding, but they do play a role as an important background when decisions are made under the Environmental Code.

457. In order to achieve these goals – legal and political – there are different types of provisions in the Environmental Code. The general provisions apply to all kinds of activities regardless of whether the activity in question is performed on land, in water, by a private individual, companies or authorities or other public bodies. Examples of generally applicable provisions are the general rules of consideration, the basic provisions on management of land and water and the environmental quality standards. For a number of specific activities, such as environmentally hazardous activities, water operations and waste management, there are special provisions. Before describing the general and specific provisions of the Code (*see* paragraphs 469–536), we will give a brief overview of the links between the Environmental Code and EU law and other (national) legislation, respectively (*see* paragraphs 458–468).

§2. Links to EU Law

458. As already mentioned, EU legislation – including *inter alia* regulations which are directly applicable and directives which are to be transformed into national legislation – has a significant impact in the field of environmental law. When applying the Environmental Code, EU law often has to be taken into consideration either through directly applicable provisions, or indirectly as a mean of interpretation of the relevant national legislation.

459. EU legislation covers several different areas of environmental law, such as nature conservancy and protection, chemicals, waste, noise, and the protection of air and water.

460. The environmental directives issued by the EU often determine minimum standards, which means that Member States are entitled to apply a higher level of this protection in their national legislations, should they so desire. An example is the Swedish national legislation on waste issues. However, in other areas – e.g., concerning the free movement of goods – EU law aims to harmonize the legislation within the entire union. A harmonized area is for instance the requirements on exhaust emission levels from automobiles, where a car which has been approved in one Member State must in principle be possible to sell and market in other Member States without any additional environmental requirements.

§3. Links to Other National Legislation

461. It must be borne in mind that not all environmental issues are exhaustively regulated within the framework of the Environmental Code. The Planning and Building Act, the Minerals Act and the Combustibles and Explosives Act constitute examples of other acts containing environmental requirements, *see* further Chapter 4 *infra*. Moreover, the application of certain individual provisions of the Environmental Code is prescribed in several other Acts, such as the Electricity Act, the Natural Gas Act, the Pipelines Act, and the Nuclear Activities Act (regarding said Acts *see* generally *supra*).

462. The relationship between such other legislation and the Environmental Code is rather complex. The principal rule is that, in addition to the provisions of the Environmental Code, the provisions of other legislation shall be applicable to activities that may cause damage or detriment to human health, the environment or other interests that are protected by the Code.[135] This means, as the main rule, a parallel application of the Environmental Code together with other legislation of the kind described.

463. For example, a measure which requires a building permit – e.g., the construction of a building for energy generation purposes – under the Planning and Building Act shall be examined under the provisions of the Planning and Building Act, *inter alia* with regard to the special rules on environmental consideration laid down in the said Act. In addition, the operations which are to be conducted in the building – e.g., the combustion of natural gas – are subject to an assessment according

135. Environmental Code, Ch. 1, s. 3.

to the Environmental Code, if such operations may cause damage or detriment human health or the environment.

464. However, with respect to the granting of licences or concessions for operations that are governed by licence or concessions requirements stipulated in other Acts, the principle of *lex specialis* normally applies. This means that a licence or concession shall be granted by the relevant authority based exclusively on the provisions of the Act containing the licence or concession requirements in question. Only if, and to the extent that, the other Act explicitly refers to the Environmental Code, provisions specifically referred to shall be applied when the concession or licence requirements are assessed.[136] The method of 'limited application' of the Environmental Code with regard to licence or concession requirements are found in several of the regulatory Acts in the energy sector.

465. Hence, as mentioned *supra*, the Electricity Act, the Natural Gas Act and the Pipelines Act all prescribe in detail the prerequisites for the granting of concessions (for high-voltage power lines, natural gas pipelines and other pipelines, respectively), but, in addition, provide that certain individual provisions of the Environmental Code (i.e., not the Environmental Code in its entirety) shall apply when assessing the concession matter, *viz.* the general rules of consideration (Chapter 2), the basic and special provisions concerning land and water management in Sweden (Chapters 3–4), and the provisions on environmental quality standards (Chapter 5, section 3 and Chapter 16, section 5). Furthermore, all three Acts refer to the Environmental Code (Chapter 6) as regards the contents of the EIA that shall be included in the different kinds of concession applications.[137] As regards, the contents of those provisions of the Environmental Code *see* generally paragraphs 469–481 *infra*.

466. The principle of *lex specialis* is laid down with respect to the licence requirements under the Nuclear Activities Act and the Radiation Protection Act too, *see* paragraphs 178–186 and 194–196 *supra*.[138] Thus, the Nuclear Activities Act contains the same references to the Environmental Code as the Electricity Act and the Pipelines Act do.[139] This is also the case with respect to the Radiation Protection Act,[140] albeit that the said Act does not refer to the general rules of consideration or the basic and special provisions concerning land and water management of the Code, as those provisions are not deemed relevant to the operations covered by the Radiation Protection Act.

467. As an exception from the rule discussed above, certain operations are subject to both a concession requirement under a special Act and a permit requirement under the Environmental Code. Such parallel concessions and permit requirements apply, for example, with respect to mining activities, which are subject to both an

---

136. B. Bengtsson et al., *Miljöbalken, en kommentar, del 1* (Nordstedts 2015).
137. Cf. the Electricity Act, Ch. 2, s. 8a, the Natural Gas Act, Ch. 2, s. 7 and the Pipelines Act, s. 4.
138. As regards the application of the Environmental Code and the Nuclear Activities Act with respect to the construction of nuclear power plants and research reactors, the legal situation is more complex; *see* Bengtsson et al., *Miljöbalken, en kommentar, del2* 17:8–17:9 (Nordstedts 2012).
139. Nuclear Activities Act, s. 5 b.
140. Radiation Protection Act, s. 22 a.

exploitation permit under the Minerals Act (*see generally* paragraphs 571–598 *infra*) and a permit requirement as an environmental hazardous activity pursuant to Chapter 9 of the Environmental Code.[141]

468. In the following, we will provide an overview of the main provisions in the Environmental Code. This overview is limited to certain aspects of the generally applicable provisions, permit requirements and other procedural issues for environmentally hazardous activities and water operations, provisions on remediation of polluted areas, water issues and third-party claims.

§4. General Provisions

I. General Rules of Consideration

469. The fundamental rule of consideration (*hänsynsregler*) of the Environmental Code (Chapter 2, section 3) is the precautionary principle, according to which anyone who pursues an activity, takes a measure or intends to do so, is obliged to take the necessary precautions to prevent or minimize damage or nuisance to human health and the environment. Precautions must be taken as soon as there is a reason to assume that an activity or a measure may cause damage or nuisance to human health or the environment.

470. The precautionary principle is supplemented by a number of other principles, many of which specify the manner in which precautionary measures should be performed. Those who conduct activities or take measures must:

- obtain the knowledge that is necessary to protect human health and the environment (Chapter 2, section 2);
- avoid the use of chemical products or biotechnical organisms if they can be replaced with less dangerous products (Chapter 2, section 6);
- locate the activities so that their purpose is achieved with a minimum of damage or nuisance to human health and the environment (Chapter 2, section 6);
- ensure that the activity is performed in accordance with their source management and eco-cycle principles, thus conserving raw materials and energy (Chapter 2, section 5); and
- use the best possible technique (Chapter 2, section 3, paragraph 1),which in combination with the reasonability assessment (*see infra*) equals to best available technique under the IED-directive.[142]

471. The above principles are supplemented by a rule of reason under which the principles must be complied with only insofar as this is not deemed *unreasonable*

141. Bengtsson et al., *Miljöbalken, en kommentar, del* (Nordstedts 2015).

142. Directive 2010/75/EU of the European Parliament and of the Council of 24 Nov. 2010 on industrial emissions (integrated pollution prevention and control). The central parts of the IED-directive will be implemented in Swedish law through the Industry Envisions Ordinance (2013:250), in force as of 18 Jun. 2013.

(Chapter 2, section 7). In practice, the application of the rule of reason is a cost-benefit assessment.[143]

472. Activities that entail certain particularly serious effects on the environment and human health may be prohibited even though all legally required protection measures have been taken. The Government may, however, grant exceptions on the basis of public interest (Chapter 2, sections 9–10).[144]

II. Basic and Special Provisions for Management of Land and Water

473. The Environmental Code provides general guidelines concerning the balance between protection and exploitation of natural resources. The main consideration should always be what constitutes 'the best use' in the public interest.

474. Under the Code's basic provisions for management of land and water (Chapter 3), certain factors must be taken into account when a change in the use of land or water is planned, *inter alia* that areas that are particularly vulnerable from an ecological point of view, to the extent possible, shall be protected against measures that may damage the natural environment, whereas areas that are particularly suitable as sites for facilities for e.g., energy production, energy distribution or other industrial activities, to the extent possible, shall be protected against measures that may be prejudicial to the establishment or use of such sites.

475. The Code's special provisions concerning land and water and water management in certain areas in Sweden (Chapter 4) outline the fundamental requirements for use of land and water and the necessary considerations for geographical areas of particular interest, such as a defined mountain, coastal areas and lake areas. For example, in areas of national interest, environmental interventions may only be undertaken where they can be implemented in a manner that does not significantly damage the natural and cultural assets of these areas.

III. Environmental Quality Standards

476. Prior to Sweden's entry into the EU in 1995, Swedish environmental law was not structured around statutory capped emissions levels or other fixed metering values with respect to the status of the environment. Rather, such levels or values have, in general, been provided in the form of non-binding (at least in the formal sense) guidelines and recommendations issued by the supervisory authorities, and this is still

143. Cf. Environmental Code, Ch. 2, s. 7. *See also* Bengtsson et al., *Miljöbalken, en kommentar, del 1* (Nordstedts 2015).

144. An example of a (controversial) application of the prohibition rule (Ch. 2, s. 9) in an energy law context is the opinion submitted to the Government by the Environmental Court in Vänersborg (Case M 45-03, opinion of 28 Apr. 2005) regarding the permissibility of the operations at Ringhals nuclear power plant.

the case in a number of areas. However, there are several Directives that set fixed environmental quality standards regarding, *inter alia*, air, water and soil quality.[145]

477. Therefore, rules on environmental quality standards (*miljökvalitetsnormer*) implementing the relevant provisions of the relevant Directives have been introduced in the Environmental Code (Chapter 5) and Ordinances issued pursuant to the Code.[146]

478. An environmental quality standard stipulates the highest permitted concentration of a pollutant in air, water, or soil, etc. within a fixed geographical area. Regional and local authorities are responsible to ensure that environmental quality standards are complied with, and shall observe the standards when they consider permits and otherwise apply the Environmental Code.[147] A permit may be revised, if the activities conducted under the permit to a significant extent are responsible for an infringement of an environmental quality standard.

479. The environmental quality standards have different legal effect depending on their definition as limit value standards or other standards. According to the Environmental Code, it is possible to impose stricter requirements for the observance of an environmental quality standard with limit values, if needed in an individual situation. Other environmental quality standards, for which limit values do not apply, must only obey the general rules of consideration to an extent considered reasonable.

480. The Government, or regional or local authorities appointed by the Government, must establish an action programme, if this is necessary to comply with an environmental quality standard.

481. These environmental quality standards implement, *inter alia*, the following Directives into Swedish law:

- The Directive of 18 July 1978 on the quality of fresh waters needing protection or improvement in order to support fish life (78/659/EEC).
- The Directive of 30 October 1979 on the quality required of shellfish waters (79/923/EEC).
- Directive 2002/3/EG of the European Parliament and of the Council of February 2002 relating to ozone in ambient air.
- Directive 2004/107/EC of the European Parliament and of the Council of 15 December 2004 relating to arsenic, cadmium, mercury, nickel and polycyclic aromatic hydrocarbons in ambient air.
- Directive 2008/50/EC of the European Parliament and of the Council of 21 May 2008 on ambient air quality and cleaner air for Europe.
- Directive 2008/56/EC of the European Parliament and of the Council of 17 June 2008 establishing a framework for community action in the field of marine environmental policy (Marine Strategy Framework Directive).

---

145. A survey over Directives containing environmental quality standards is given in the preparatory works to the Environmental Code, *see* Prop. 1997/98:45 I, pp. 247 et seq.
146. For instance Ordinance (2004:660) on Water Quality Management, Ordinance (2004:675) on Environmental Quality Standards for Noise, Ordinance (2010:477) on Environmental Quality Standards for Ambient Air, and Ordinance (2006:44) on Environmental Quality Standards for Fish and Bivalve Waters.
147. Prop. 2009/10:184.

- Directive 2008/105/EC of the European Parliament and of the Council of 16 December 2008 on environmental quality standards in the field of water policy.

§5. Permit Requirements for Environmental Hazardous Activities

I. The Concept of 'Environmental Hazardous Activities'

482. Under the Environmental Code, a number of activities require a permit issued by the relevant authority or court. In this overview, we focus on environmentally hazardous activities related to energy generation and other energy processes, and on water operations, which are relevant, e.g., with respect to the construction and operation of hydropower plants, laying of pipelines in water, offshore wind power plants and construction measures which encompass diversion of groundwater, *see* paragraphs 483–505 *infra*.

483. The legal framework regarding environmental hazardous activities are laid down in Chapter 9 of the Environmental Code, and supplemented primarily by the Ordinance (1998:899) concerning Environmentally Hazardous Activities and the Protection of Public Health (henceforth the 'Ordinance on Environmentally Hazardous Activities') and the Ordinance (2013:251) on Environmental Assessment.

484. The Code (Chapter 9, section 1) defines environmentally hazardous activities as:

(1) the discharge of wastewater, solid matter or gas from land, buildings or structures onto land or into water areas or groundwater;
(2) any use of land, buildings or structures that entails a risk of nuisance to human health or the environment due to discharges or emissions or to pollution of land, air, water areas or groundwater; or
(3) any use of land, buildings or structures that may cause a nuisance to the surroundings due to noise, vibration, light, ionizing or non-ionizing radiation or similar impact.

485. The concept 'activity' should be construed extensively. For example, storage of hazardous substances (even without the knowledge of the 'operator'/ landowner) may be deemed to be such an activity.[148]

II. Permit and Notification Requirements

A. General

486. In the Ordinance on Environmental Assessment, the environmental hazardous activities that require a permit are listed. Hence, it should be noted that not all environmentally hazardous (according to the definition above) activities require a

148. Bengtsson et al., *Miljöbalken, en kommentar, del 1* (Nordstedts 2015).

permit. The Ordinance also contains those activities that may be conducted after a notification to the local authorities. .

487. Permit requirements depend on the type of activity in question and the size and environmental impact of the activity. Different activities are classified for this purposed as A, B or C activities in the Ordinance. Those environmental hazardous activities that require a permit from the Land and Environmental Court (in general, industries and other activities having a major impact on the environment) are denoted as 'A' in the Ordinance. The 'B' activities comprise those activities for which permits are granted by the County Administrative Board. Further, the 'C' activities are subject to a notification duty only (to the relevant municipality).

488. However, even where a permit is not required under the Ordinance on Environmental Assessment, the supervisory authority may in individual cases order an operator to apply for a permit where the activity involves the risk of significant pollution or other significant detriment to human health or the environment (Environmental Code, Chapter 9, section 6, paragraph 2).

489. In addition, a person or entity who pursues or intends to pursue an environmentally hazardous activity may apply for a permit for the activity in accordance with the Code even where such a permit is not compulsory (Chapter 9 section 6, paragraph 3). The ground for a permit application on a 'voluntary' basis is normally that a permit provides an increased security for the permit holder to operate his activity in accordance with the permit and its conditions without facing the risk of injunctions and prohibitions from the supervisory authority as long as the permit is in effect, *see* further paragraphs 524–527 *infra*.

490. Alterations of activities may require a permit; however, the permit may be limited to include only the alteration in question. No assessment will be made in case of alterations that have no harmful effects on human health or the environment.[149] Activities that were commenced before the duty to obtain a permit was introduced have also been made subject to the permit obligation. This also applies to activities that under the previous rules were exempted from permit requirements.

B. Energy-Related Processes Subject to Permit Requirements

491. Under the Ordinance on Environmental Assessment, *inter alia* the following energy-related activities[150] are subject to a permit or notification requirement, according to A, B or C classifications referred to *supra*:

(1) Nuclear power plants and other nuclear reactors (A).

---

149. Ordinance (2013:251) on Environmental Assessment, Ch. 1, s. 4.

150. Please note that this is a summary for overview purposes, which does not cover all energy-related activities. Moreover, certain activity descriptions may have been shortened and simplified. For the exact descriptions of the respective activities subject to permit requirements, reference is made to the Ordinance on Environmental Hazardous Activities. Please also note that the list on activities that require a permit under the Environmental Code will be set out (and to some extent changed) in the new Ordinance on Environmental Assessment (2013:251) which enters into force on 18 Jun. 2013. Most energy-related activities are listed in Chs 21–22 of this new ordinance.

(2) Dismantling and decommissioning of nuclear power plants and nuclear reactors (A).
(3) Facility for combustion/incineration with a total installed supplied power of more than 300 MW (A).
(4) Facility for combustion/incineration with a total installed supplied power of more than 50 MW (B).
(5) Combustion facility with a total installed power of more than 500 kW, using other than only fuel oil or fuel gas as energy source (C).
(6) Combustion facility with an installed power of more than 10 MW, using only fuel oil or fuel gas as energy source (C).
(7) Gas-turbine plant with a maximum total installed supplied power of 20 MW (C).
(8) Two and more wind power turbines located together (wind farm) for which the height of each of the turbines including the rotor blades are more than 150 metres (B).
(9) Seven or more wind power turbines located together (wind farm) and each of the turbines including the rotor blades are higher than 120 metres (B).
(10) A wind farm, including rotor blades, higher than 50 metres (C).
(11) Two or more wind power turbines located together (wind farm), and is not subject to a permit requirement (C).
(12) A wind power turbine located together with another wind power turbine, if not taken in operation simultaneously.
(13) Heat pump or cooling plant for the transfer of heat energy – by means other than via a public water supply – from or into the ground, a watercourse, lake or other body of water, or from groundwater or waste water, with a total effect of more than 10 MW (C).
(14) Facility for storage of natural gas with an amount exceeding 50 million cubic metres per year (B).
(15) Facility for storage or handling of gaseous or liquid petrochemical products, oils, petroleum products or combustible gases if the storage has a capacity storage of more than 50,000 tonnes or if more than 500,000 tonnes are handled per year (B).
(16) Facility for storage or handling of gaseous or liquid petrochemical products, oils, petroleum products or combustible gases if it is stored more than 5,000 tonnes or if more than 500,000 tonnes are handled per year (B).
(17) Deep drilling (C).
(18) Mine or mining of coal within certain geographical areas of national interest specified in Chapter 4, section 5 of the Environmental Code (A).
(19) Mine or mining of coal in other areas, including test-mining (B).
(20) Extraction of raw petroleum or natural gas within certain geographical areas of national interest specified in Chapter 4, section 5 of the Environmental Code (A).
(21) Extraction of raw petroleum or natural gas within other areas (B).
(22) Industrial production of coal briquettes or brown coal (C).
(23) Mine or mining of ore, mineral or coal (A).
(24) Test-mining including treatment or extraction of ore, mineral or coal (B).
(25) Facility for manufacture of coke, transfer of coal or shale to gas or liquid or graphite manufacturing (B).

(26) Facility for manufacture of products of coal (B).
(27) Facility for annual production of more than 150,000 cubic metre gaseous fuel (B).
(28) Facility for annual production of less than 150,000 cubic metre gaseous fuel (C).
(29) Mineral oil or natural gas refinery (A).
(30) Facility for treatment, processing or storage of nuclear fuel (A).
(31) Facility for handling reprocessing, stockpiling or final storage of nuclear fuel, nuclear waste or other radioactive waste (A).

In addition, several activities related to the handling (storage, intermediate storage, treatment, recycling, etc.) of hazardous and non-hazardous waste are subject to permit or notification requirements under the Environmental Code.

§6. Permit Requirements for Water Operations

I. The Concept of 'Water Operations'

492. Under Chapter 11 of the Environmental Code, water operations are – with a few exceptions – subject to a permit or notification requirement. Permits for water operations are granted by the Land and Environmental Court while notifications are made to the County Administrative Boards.

493. Under the Code (Chapter 11, section 2), water operations include:

- the construction, alteration, repair and removal of dams or other water constructions, filling and piling in water areas, the removal of water from or digging, blasting and cleansing in water areas, as well as other measures whose purpose is to change the depth or position of the water;
- the diversion of groundwater and the erection of structures for this purpose;
- recharging of groundwater and the erection of structures and other measures for this purpose; and
- land drainage.

494. Water operations are subject to permit requirement, unless the operations only need to be notified or otherwise is stipulated in the Code. A permit may be applied voluntarily (Chapter 11, section 1). The operations that are subject to notification are specified in the Ordinance (1998:1388) on Water Operations.

495. The permit requirement does not apply if it is obvious that neither public nor private interests are harmed by the impact of the water operations on the water conditions (Chapter 11, section 12). However, this exception is seldom applicable, unless the water activity in question is insignificant. Certain other defined activities –*inter alia* the erection of structures for heat generation – are also exempt from the permit requirement (Chapter 11, section 11).

II. Special Conditions Applying to Water Operations

496. In order for a water operation to be permitted, the Code provides that the following special conditions must be fulfilled (Chapter 11, sections 6–8).

497. First, water operations may only be undertaken, if the benefits to the public and private interests exceed the costs and damage associated with them, i.e., a cost-benefit analysis of each individual project is envisaged.

498. Second, water operations shall be implemented in such a way as not be prejudicial to other activities which are likely to involve the same water source in the future and which serve important public or private purposes.

499. Third, persons or entities who intend to carry out water operations that may be detrimental to fishing must, at their own expense, make and in future maintain any arrangements that are necessary for the passage of fish or the sustainability of fishing, supply water for this purpose and comply with any other conditions that may be necessary in the context of the operations to protect fishing in the water in which the water operations are carried on or in adjacent water areas.

III. Simultaneous Application of Chapters 9 and 11 of the Environmental Code

500. An activity or measure can be subject to both a permit requirement for water operations under Chapter 11 of the Code and a permit requirement for environmental hazardous activities under Chapter 9 of the Code, *see* paragraphs 482–491 *supra*. For example, the erection of a large combustion plant, where divesting of groundwater may be required in the process of the construction work, has to be assessed under the rules for environmental hazardous activities as well as the rules for water operations. In such cases, the two permit matters are in general cumulated and handled by the Environmental Court in order to enable a joint assessment of the project and to avoid conflicting decisions or judgments by different instances.

501. As regards water operations related to hydropower plants and dams, *see specifically* paragraphs 140–175 *supra*.

IV. Water Operations Assessed under Special Procedures

502. Certain water operations are assessed separately under special Acts and procedures. This applies *inter alia* with respect to construction of bridges, roads and railways. In the energy sector, such separate assessments of water operations are made in concession matters regarding the construction of pipelines under the Natural Gas Act and the Pipelines Act, where such pipelines are constructed in water areas or otherwise involve water operations.

503. Moreover, the Government may assess water operations in connection with its permissibility assessment of certain major projects –*inter alia* the construction of large combustion plants, hydropower plants and wind farms – under Chapter 17 of the Code *see* paragraphs 514–517 *infra*.

504. Water operations that have been assessed under such separate procedures shall only be subject to a limited permissibility assessment under the Environmental Code. Thus, If the Government has imposed water operations as a condition for another operation which falls under the Government's permissibility assessment under Chapter 17 of the Code, or if a concession has been granted for a pipeline pursuant to the Pipelines Act or the Natural Gas Act, the Code stipulates that, among other special assessment procedures for water operations, the permissibility for the connected water operations shall not be assessed by the Land and Environmental Court. The Court shall grant the water operations permit for the operation in question, subject only to an assessment of to the provisions of Chapter 2, section 9 of the Code concerning very adverse effects to human health or the environment,[151] *see also* paragraphs 469–472 *supra*.

505. It should be noted that, according to court practice, this exception regarding a limited assessment of water operations does not apply to concessions for electricity power lines, which are constructed in water areas.[152]

§7. Permit Application and EIA Procedure

I. Permit Application

506. An operator of an environmentally hazardous activity that requires a permit must file an *application* for such permit with the relevant Land and Environmental Court (A-activities) or County Administrative Board (B-activities) depending on the size and environmental impact of the operation in question, *see* paragraphs 486–491 *supra*.

507. An application for water operations shall be submitted to the Land and Environmental Court (Environmental Code, Chapter 11, section 9).

508. An application for a permit must contain information on the environmental impact of the operations; undertakings to reduce this impact and various other information (*see* Chapter 22, section 1).

II. Environmental Impact Assessment

509. A permit application – both as regards environmental hazardous activities and water operations – must be accompanied by an EIA.

510. The EIA-provisions of the Environmental Code (Chapter 6) implements the EIA-Directive 2011/92/EU,[153] which codifies the previous Directive 85/337/EEC

151. Environmental Code, Ch. 11, s. 23.
152. The Superior Environmental Court (MÖD), case no. M 593-99, decisions of 22 Jun. 1999 and 28 Jun. 1999, SM10, regarding a power cable from Sweden to Poland.
153. Directive 2011/92/EU of the European Parliament and of the Council of 13 Dec. 2011 on the assessment of the effects of certain public and private projects on the environment.

and its amendments.[154] The EIA-Directive has been amended by Directive 2014/52/EU.[155]

511. The purpose of an EIA is to identify, describe and provide a general assessment of the direct and indirect effects of an activity on humans, flora, climate, etc. The EIA procedure includes consultations with authorities and private parties that are particularly affected by the activity covered by the application.

512. Under the Environmental Code, an EIA shall include the following information:

- a description of the activity;
- a description of measures planned with a view to avoiding, mitigating or remedying adverse effects caused by the activity;
- information needed to establish and assess the main impact of the activity on human health, animals, plants, etc.;
- a description of possible alternative locations for the activity and alternative designs, as well as the reasons for the chosen alternative and a description of the consequences if the activity or measure is not implemented; and
- a non-technical summary.

513. The relevant permit authority decides on whether or not the EIA satisfies the legal requirements.

§8. Assessment of Permissibility of the Government in Certain Cases

514. Under the Environmental Code (Chapter 17), the Government shall consider the permissibility of certain operations of national interest. Certain activities are subject to an obligatory assessment by the Government, and as regards the energy sector such obligation applies to nuclear installations and plants for the extraction of uranium-bearing materials or other substances that can be used for the production of nuclear fuel (Chapter 17, section 1, paragraph 1).

515. The Government may reserve for itself the right to assess the permissibility for an operation that is not subject to an obligatory assessment by the Government, if the activity is expected to be large or have a considerable impact on the interests to be protected by the Environmental Code, if it may harm natural values in protected areas or is subject to the provisions in Chapter 4, section 6, third paragraph of the Code (hydroelectric power).

516. At the request of a municipal authority, the Government shall reserve for itself the power to assess the permissibility of certain new activities. This applies in particular to the following operations in the energy sector:

154. Council Directive 85/337/EEC of 27 Jun. 1985 on the assessment of the effects of certain public and private projects on the environment.

155. Directive 2014/52/EU of the European Parliament and of the Council of 16 Apr. 2014 amending Directive 2011/92/EU on the assessment of the effects of certain public and private projects on the environment.

- crude oil refineries;
- combustion plants with an input power not less than 200 MW;
- wind farms that are subject to a permit requirement; consisting of clusters of three or more wind turbines with a total output of not less than 10 MW;
- facilities for the storage of not less than 50 million m^3 of natural gas;
- mining activities in certain geographical areas defined as being of national interest;
- hydroelectric power plants designed for an output of not less than 20 MW;
- water regulation facilities with a water reservoir capacity of not less than 100 million cubic metre per year or 10 million cubic metre per week; and
- the construction of platforms for offshore oil or gas extraction.

517. The Government's assessment shall take place as a step in the decision-making process under the Environmental Code. The applicant applies to the relevant permit authority, usually the Environmental Court. The permit authority handles the case in an ordinary manner and subsequently refers the matter over to the Government with its opinion. The Government decides if the activity should be permitted or not. The permit authority is bound by the Government's decision in this respect but can, if the permit is granted, impose conditions.

§9. Permit Conditions and General Requirements for Granting a Permit

518. Under the Environmental Code, permits are generally issued for a limited period of time, but could also be granted without any time limit (Chapter 16, section 2, paragraph 1).

519. Permits under the Environmental Code are normally issued subject to a number of conditions set forth in the permit (Chapter 16, section 2, paragraph 2). In case of environmentally hazardous activities, conditions may, for example, concern the use of a particular purification equipment, that emission levels and noise levels are not exceeded, that chemicals will be handled in particular manner, and that the operator of the activity provides a security for the expenses for site remediation and other reinstatement measures. Permits for water operations may contain several other conditions, e.g., to implant fish in rivers to compensate damage on fishery.

520. Permits may be conditioned upon a provided security for the costs incurred by the restoration of an environmental damage or other remedying measures due to the activities. The security is assessed by the supervising authority (Chapter 16, section 3).

521. Permits for wind farms may only be granted if the municipality concerned has approved such activity (Chapter 16, section 4). Thus, municipalities have a veto right as regards wind farms planned to be located within their respective municipal area.

522. Permits may be refused on the grounds that a party has not complied with conditions of previous permits (Chapter 16, section 6).

523. As regards certain additional conditions which apply for the granting of a permit for water operations, *see* paragraphs 496–499 *supra*.

§10. Validity, Duration and Reconsiderations of Permits, Etc.

524. Under the Environmental Code, a permit that has gained legal force is valid against all other parties – i.e., in relation to the State (acting through the environmental authorities), the permit holder itself and third parties – as far as the matters examined in the permit judgment or decision are concerned (Chapter 24, section 1).

525. The legal force of the permit means *inter alia* that an action for the prohibition of an environmentally hazardous activity or for an injunction upon on a permit holder (who acts in conformity with the permit) cannot be granted.[156] This principle applies both to actions by a private third party[157] and to actions by the supervisory authority,[158] even though it does not prevent the supervisory authority from issuing a summary order or prohibition in order to avoid health effects or serious damage to the environment. Thus, a permit provides a security for the permit holder. In general, he does not have to fear that the authorities impose additional environmental requirements to his operations with respect to matters that have been examined in the permit matter.[159]

526. The permit authority may completely or partially revoke a permit and prohibit continued activity in various situations. This may be the case, *inter alia*, if the applicant has misled the permit authority, if the permit conditions attached to the permit are not complied with and the non-compliance is not of minor significance, or if nuisance of substantial importance arises that was not anticipated when the permit was granted (Environmental Code, Chapter 24, section 3).

527. The permit or conditions of the permit may also be reconsidered. Reconsideration may take place after ten years or, in some cases, within a shorter period of time (Environmental Code, Chapter 24, section 5).

§11. Transfer of Permits

528. A permit for environmental hazardous activities under Chapter 9 of the Environmental Code, as well as a permit for water operations under Chapter 11 of the Environmental Code, is linked to the operation as such and not to the permit holder. Therefore, the sale and purchase of the operations (i.e., a hydropower plant) does not require any consent from the authorities, nor does it trigger any review of the permit or the permit conditions.

529. With respect to the transfer of operations of environmental hazardous activities, which are subject to a permit or notification requirement, a new operator of such an activity must notify the supervisory authority of the transfer.[160]

530. Certain other permits, e.g., exploration permits and exploitation concessions under the Minerals Act as well as permits under the Nuclear Activities Act are, however,

---

156. P.H. Lindblom, *Miljöprocess II* 680 (Iustus Förlag 2002).
157. Such an action can be initiated pursuant to the Environmental Code, Ch. 32, s. 12.
158. Environmental Code, Ch. 26, s. 9, para. 3.
159. Cf. Prop. 1997/98:45 II, p. 252.
160. Ordinance on Environmental Hazardous Activities, s. 32.

linked to the permit holder. Where such permits are transferable, the transfer generally requires the consent of the permit authority or the supervisory authority. The same principle applies *inter alia* with respect to the transfer of concessions under the Electricity Act, the Natural Gas Act and the Pipelines Act, under which Acts a consent (by the Energy Agency or the Government) for the transfer of the concession in question is required.[161]

§12. Waste

531. Several energy processes give rise to different waste products, for example ashes from combustion or waste oil.

532. The concept of waste under the Environmental Code is in accordance with that of the EU Waste Directive 2008/98/EEC.[162] For the implementation of new EU provisions on waste, new rules on waste were introduced in the Code (Chapter 15) and a new waste ordinance[163] was adopted in 2011.

533. Under the Waste Directive and the Environmental Code, waste is defined as any substance or object which the holder discards or intends or is required to discard (Chapter 15, section 1). The Directive and the Code also contains definition of by-product, which is a substance or object, resulting from a production process, the primary aim of which is not the production of that item but is not to be regarded as waste under certain conditions.

534. The Environmental Code makes a distinction between hazardous waste and other waste. Hazardous waste is defined and/or listed in the Waste Ordinance. A number of activities concerning hazardous waste, *inter alia* the disposal, incineration and storage of such waste, are defined as environmentally hazardous activities under Chapter 9 of the Environmental Code and are subject to a permit requirement under said provisions, *see generally* paragraphs 486–490, 491 *supra*.

535. Management of waste containing PCB – a substance which has been commonly used *inter alia* in transformers and power condensers – is subject to special provisions under the Ordinance (1998:122) on Disposal of PCB, which contains detailed provisions on disposal of PCB. Under the Ordinance, PCB-contagious waste may only be disposed of through certain types of biologic or physicochemical treatment or incineration. Further, the Ordinance prescribes that anyone who disposes of PCB must keep a record and disposal must take place without delay.

536. In addition to the permit requirement referred to *supra*, plants for incineration of waste are covered by special provisions pursuant to the Ordinance (2002:1060) on Incineration of Waste. This Ordinance contains detailed provisions on the operation of incineration plants and limit values for emissions to air and water. These provisions implement the provision of Directive 2000/76/EC on the Incineration of Waste.

---

161. Cf. Minerals Act, Ch. 6, s. 1, Electricity Act Ch. 2, s. 16, Natural Gas Act Ch. 2, s. 13 and Pipelines Act, s. 13.

162. Directive 2008/98/EC of the European Parliament and of the Council of 19 Nov. 2008 on waste and repealing certain Directives.

163. Waste Ordinance (2011:927).

§13. Remediation of Polluted Areas

537. Energy processes may cause pollution. In paragraphs 538–547 *infra*, we briefly address the provisions of the Environmental Code which deal with remediation of polluted areas, liability for private claims due to polluting activities, as well as certain insurance matters.

538. The Environmental Code (Chapter 10) contains provisions on remediation of polluted areas. Those provisions are applicable to land and water, and buildings and structures, which are polluted to such an extent as to entail a risk for damage or nuisance to human health or the environment. These provisions can be summarized as follows.

539. The overriding principle of the liability regime under the Code is the 'polluter pays principle' (which is expressed in Chapter 2, section 8). In somewhat simplified terms, those who have conducted a polluting activity – i.e., the operator(s) – after 30 June 1969 may be liable for remedying the area which has been contaminated by the activity (Chapter 10, section 2).[164]

540. If two or more parties have conducted the polluting activity in succession, the liability is joint and several (Chapter 10, section 6, paragraph 1). Hence, the supervisory authority may choose to hold one of the parties, in practice generally the current operator, liable for all remediation measures. This party may thereafter be entitled to recover costs from other, previous or current, operators at the site in question.

541. However, the liability under the above-mentioned provisions is subject to a rule of reason (Chapter 10, section 6, paragraph 2). This test of reasonableness takes into account *inter alia* the period of time that has elapsed since the area became polluted, historic compliance with permits and other rules, and any other relevant circumstances.

542. If a liable operator cannot be established or if he is not able to perform the necessary remediation measures, anyone who, after 31 December 1998, has acquired or acquires a polluted area (property unit) with knowledge of a contamination within the area in question may be held liable for reasonable remediation measures. The same applies if the purchaser should have known about the contamination (Chapter 10, section 3).

§14. Liability for Private Claims

543. Under Chapter 32 of the Environmental Code, operators of a polluting activity, who are owners or site-leaseholders (*tomträttsinnehavare*) of a property on which the polluting activity take place, are liable for pollution outside the property. Others, who use the property in the course of their business – such as tenants and contractors, can also be held liable. The liability comprises actual damages on property or to persons, as well as pure economic loss (*ren förmögenhetsskada*) which is of any significance (Chapter 32, sections 1 and 6–8).

544. If the damage has not been caused by intent or negligence, the operator is however only liable to the extent the pollution should not reasonably be tolerated taking into account the environmental conditions in the specific geographical area in

164. This provision shall be read in conjunction with the Promulgation Act to the Environmental Code (*Lag om införande av miljöbalken, SFS 1998:811*), s. 8.

question or generally (Chapter 32, section 1). This means that the operator has a strict liability for polluting activities which are not deemed so tolerable.

545. The operator's liability encompasses pollution to water and groundwater, changes in the level of the groundwater, pollution to air, pollution to soil, noise, vibrations or any damage similar to the above. The latter includes pollution causing harm to aesthetic values and certain psychological effects. The burden of proof for the plaintiff – as regards the cause of the damage – has been eased in comparison to ordinary tort law (Chapter 32, section 3).

546. Damage according to the Environmental Code also encompasses pollution caused by blasts and excavation works, if the operator has not taken the necessary precautionary measures (Chapter 32, section 4).

547. Liability for pollution caused by radiation or electric current is not covered by Chapter 32 of the Environmental Code. Such liability falls under provisions of the Nuclear Activities Act and the Electricity Act, respectively.

§15. Land and Environmental Courts

548. Prior to the entry into force of the Environmental Code, larger permits matters were tried by the Franchise Board for Environmental Protection (*Koncessionsnämnden för miljöskydd*).

549. Under the Environmental Code, regional land and environmental Courts have been created. There are five land and environmental Courts which are part of the District Courts in Nacka, Vänersborg, Växjö, Umeå and Östersund.[165]

550. The Environmental Code (Chapter 21 sections 1–2) also regulates procedural law in the environmental law domain cases decided by the land and environmental court as first instance. The cases are divided between either application cases (*ansökningsmål*) or summons cases (*stämningsmål*). Application cases include, *inter alia*, cases on permits for environmentally hazardous activities and water operations. Example of summons applications is cases for compensation for environmental damage. Different procedural rules apply to these two types of cases.

551. In the settling of cases and matters, the judicial competencies as well as expert knowledge are a part of the assessment, and thus judges adjudicate alongside technical advisors (having technical or scientific knowledge) and special members of court.

§16. Appeals

552. In cases where a land and environmental court is the first instance, appeals are made to the Land and Environmental Court of Appeal (*Mark- och miljööverdomstolen*), which comprises a part of the Svea Court of Appeal (*Svea hovrätt*).The last instance under the Environmental Code is the Supreme Court (*Högsta domstolen*). However,

165. Act (2010:921) on Land and Environmental Courts and Ordinance (2010:984) on the Judiciary Districts of the Land and Environmental Courts.

in practice, very few cases end up in the Supreme Court, as there is a strict screening process before cases are allowed before the Supreme Court.

553. Where the County Administrative Board is the first instance, decisions may be appealed to the land and environmental court. In such cases, the last instance is the Land and Environmental Court of Appeal (Chapter 19, section 1).

554. Decisions taken by municipal authorities may be appealed to the County Administrative Board. The third instance in such cases is the land and environmental court and the highest is the Land and Environmental Court of Appeal (Chapter 19, section 1).

555. In most cases, judgments and decisions under the Environmental Code can be appealed by anyone concerned by the judgment or decision, if the deciding body ruled against his interests. In some cases, government authorities, municipal regulatory authorities and others may also appeal a decision. A permit decision may also be appealed by certain well-established non-profit organizations for the protection of the environment (Chapter 16, sections 12–13).

§17. Supervision

556. Under the Environmental Code (Chapter 26), the task of the supervisory authorities is to inspect and follow-up any human activities that may have an impact on human health or the environment. The supervision must ensure that such activities comply with the provisions of the Environmental Code (including any ordinances and authority regulations issued under the Code), permits and other decisions taken under the Code. In order to do so, the supervisory authority may issue orders and prohibitions. Such orders and prohibitions are subject to a principle of proportionality; the supervisory authority may not order more onerous measures than necessary in the individual case.

557. Different authorities supervise different types of activities, but in general municipal or regional authorities conduct supervision. Detailed provisions regarding supervision are set out by the Ordinance (1998:900) on Supervision under the Environmental Code.

558. The role of governmental authorities, such as the Swedish Environmental Protection Agency (*Naturvårdsverket*), is generally restricted to providing guidelines to local and regional authorities.

559. Monitoring compliance is not only a question for the environmental authorities. Under the Environmental Code, most operators of environmentally hazardous activities must continually plan and control their activities with a view to prevent damage and nuisance to human health or the environment (operator's control). Furthermore, operators of environmentally hazardous activities that require a permit must submit an environmental report annually to the supervisory authority (Chapter 26, sections 19–20). Detailed provisions regarding the operator's control are set out in the Ordinance (1998:901) on operator's self-monitoring.

§18. Environmental Sanction Charges and Penal Provisions

560. An operator, who fails to observe ordinances or regulations issued under the Environmental Code, or who conducts activities without a requisite permit or notification, can be held liable to pay an environmental sanction charge. The charge is imposed even if the violation in question has not occurred intentionally or by negligence. It is not relevant whether the business operator has had any economic gain from the violation or if the violation involved any nuisance in the particular case (Chapter 30).

561. Only violations listed in the Ordinance (2012:259) on Environmental Charges result in such charges. The Ordinance contains detailed descriptions of the violations that make environmental charges payable. Charges currently range from SEK 1,000 to SEK 1,000,000.

562. Further, a number of acts are criminalized under the Environmental Code (Chapter 29) – e.g., intentional or negligent causing of pollution or other damage to the environment, intentional or negligent breach of permit requirements, obstruction of environmental monitoring and supervision and inadequate environmental information.

563. In addition to the above general penal provisions, the non-compliance of a number of other environmental ordinances, authority regulations and permit requirements constitute criminal offences under the Code. Penalties normally range from fines to two years of imprisonment. For crimes conducted in industrial and commercial activities, a company may be imposed company fines up to an amount of SEK 10 million (Criminal Code, Chapter 36).

Chapter 3. Mining Regime

§1. General Overview

564. Since the beginning of the eighteenth century, Swedish mining legislation has been based on a mining-claim system whereby the person that first discovered a mineral resource in principle was entitled to obtain an exclusive right to explore and exploit the deposit in question.

565. Under current legislation, the right to explore and exploit mineral resources in Sweden is regulated by comprehensive regulatory framework. The main statute is the Minerals Act (*Minerallag, SFS 1991:45*), as supplemented by the Minerals Ordinance (1992:285) issued by the Government under the Act.

566. The Minerals Act is based on a concession system. The principle behind the concession system is that the right to explore and exploit a mineral deposit is granted following an assessment procedure by the authorities. The Minerals Act does, however, retain many of the principles of the mining-claim system.

567. For the purpose of exploiting natural resources, exploration of the seabed and subsoil, in public waters as well as outside the territorial waters of the Swedish economic zone is subject to the provisions of the Continental Shelf Act (*Lag om kontinentalsockeln, SFS 1966:314*). Additional provisions on the exploitation of natural resources and erection of structures within Sweden's economic zone are set out in the Act on Sweden's Economic Zone (*Lag om Sveriges ekonomiska zon, SFS 1992:1140*).

568. The exploration and exploitation of peat deposits for the purpose of generating energy is governed by the Act on Certain Peat Deposits (*Lag om vissa torvfyndigheter, SFS 1985:620*).

569. Other relevant legislation with respect to exploration and exploitation of minerals are found in the Environmental Code, the Planning and Building Act and the Act concerning Cultural Heritage Act Management. Moreover, special provisions in the Nuclear Activities Act and the Radiation Protection Act apply with respect to radioactive substances. More detailed descriptions of said acts are found in Chapter 2, *infra*, and in Part I, Chapter 3 *supra*.

570. A revision of the Minerals Act was made in 2005. The revision aimed, among other things, at strengthening the position of the property owner and the environmental interest in relation to the mineral (exploitation) interest.[166]

166. *See* Prop. 2004/05:40.

§2. Minerals Act

I. Exploration Permit

571. The Minerals Act lists a number of mineral substances (so-called concession minerals) that are subject to the provisions of the Act (Chapter 1, section 1). Among those of the concession minerals listed, certain are of interest particular for energy generation or other energy-related processes. Such concession minerals include alum shale (shale gas), uranium, coal, oil and gaseous hydrocarbons. However, none of said substances is currently subject to any commercial exploitation in Sweden, although a number of exploration permits for these minerals have been issued. Other concession minerals, in particular iron, are won in a large scale.

572. Those who would like to explore a certain area for concession minerals covered by the Minerals Act must obtain an exploration permit (*undersökningstillstånd*) from the Mining Inspector (*Bergmästaren*). The permit requirement applies to exploration work on land owned by third parties. The property owner is entitled to explore his own land for concession minerals without any permit requirement, except in respect of certain concession minerals, *inter alia* oil and gaseous hydrocarbons where an exploration permit must be granted also for the property owner (Chapter 1, section 4 and Chapter 3, section 2).

573. An exploration permit is granted for a specific area where a successful discovery is likely to be made. It should be of suitable shape and size and no larger than may be assumed can be explored by the permit holder in an appropriate manner. An exploration permit shall be granted, if there is reason to assume that exploration in the area can lead to the discovery of a concession mineral and the applicant has the possibility and intention to conduct appropriate exploration. A permit for exploration with regard to *inter alia* oil or gaseous hydrocarbons may only be granted to a person who can prove that he or she is suitable to carry out such exploration work (Chapter 2, section 2).

574. An exploration permit shall be issued with the conditions which are deemed required for the protection of private and public interests (e.g., environmental protection measures), and shall include an obligation for the holder of the permit to provide security for the damage and encroachment (*intrång*) that the work can cause to the property owner (Chapter 2, section 10).

575. In case of competition between several applicants with regard to the same area, the applicant who first submitted an application has precedence (Chapter 2, section 3).

576. An exploration permit is valid for a period of three years from the date of issue. Thereafter, it may be extended by another period of up to a maximum of three years, if suitable (*ändamålsenligt*) exploration work has been carried out during the first period. The same is valid if the permit holder has plausible excuses for exploration not yet having been carried out but nonetheless shows that it is likely that the area will be explored during the period referred to in the application. In special cases, the period of validity may be further extended for a maximum of four years. In exceptional cases, it is possible to extend the permit still further, but not for more than a total of five years. This means that the longest possible valid period for an exploration permit is fifteen years (Chapter 2, sections 5–8).

577. An exploration permit is linked to the permit holder. The transfer of an exploration permit is therefore subject to approval by the Local Mining Inspector. An approval is given if the receiver of the exploration permit does not obviously lack the possibility or intention of conducting appropriate exploration within the area. If an exploration permit concerning oil and gaseous hydrocarbons is transferred, the transferee must also prove that it is suitable to carry out such exploration work (Chapter 6, section 1 and Chapter 2, section 2).

II. Exploration Work

578. The holder of an exploration permit is entitled to carry out exploration work within the permit area. Before commencing the exploration work, the holder of an exploration permit is obliged to provide security for the damage and encroachment (*intrång*) that the work can cause to the property owner (Chapter 3, section 3, paragraph 3).

579. The permit holder may use existing roads to and within the area. Upon receipt of a separate permission from the Mining Inspector, the permit holder may also utilize land in order to build an essential road leading to, or within, the area. The work shall be so carried out as to cause the least possible damage and encroachment (Chapter 3, section 3).

580. Exploration work must be carried out in accordance with a valid work plan, which *inter alia* shall contain a description of the exploration work and a time plan for the work. The work plan can be challenged by the property owner within three weeks from his receipt hereof. In such case, the work plan will be assessed by the Mining Inspector, whose decision regarding the work plan can be appealed to a Land and Environmental Court (Chapter 3, section 5–5a and Chapter 16, section 1).

581. Exploration work is prohibited in certain areas, *inter alia* within National Parks or Nature Reserves, or subject to additional permit requirement (by the County Administrative Board or the Mining Inspector) within certain other areas, e.g., protected mountain areas and near public highways, residential areas, industrial plants or within areas covered by detailed development plans or area regulations (Chapter 3, sections 6–7).

III. Exploitation Concession

582. Under the Minerals Act, the exploitation of a mineral deposit is subject to an exploitation concession (*bearbetningskoncession*) which may be granted by the Mining Inspector or, in certain cases, the Government (Chapter 1, section 4 and Chapter 8, sections 1–2).

583. In case of competition between several applicants with regard to the same area, the holder of an exploration permit for that area has precedence (Chapter 4, section 3).

584. An exploitation concession shall be granted if a mineral deposit has been found which can presumably be exploited economically, and the location and the nature of the deposit does not make it inappropriate that the applicant is granted an exploitation concession, and with respect to oil and natural gas, the applicant is considered appropriate for the exploitation of the deposit. Moreover, an exploitation concession must not be granted in conflict with a detailed development plan or area regulations pursuant to the Planning and Building Act. However, minor deviations, which do not contravene overall purpose of the plan or regulations, may be accepted. The Environmental Code is applicable to matters concerning the granting of a concession, which means *inter alia* that an EIA shall be contained in an application for a concession. (Chapter 4, section 2).

585. An exploitation concession shall be combined with such conditions as are necessary in order to protect the public interest or individual rights or to explore and exploit the mineral deposit in a suitable manner (Chapter 4, section 5).

586. An exploitation concession is valid for a period of twenty-five years. If regular exploitation continues by then, the concession is extended automatically for another ten years. Otherwise, the concession may be extended for another ten years under certain qualifying circumstances (Chapter 4, sections 7–11).

587. An exploitation concession is linked to the concession holder. The transfer of an exploitation concession is therefore subject to a consent by the Mining Inspector. A consent may be given, if the location and nature of the deposit does not make it inappropriate that the concession is transferred to the transferee, and the transferee can prove that it is suitable to carry out the exploitation of the deposit (Chapter 6, section 1).

588. There are no restrictions to foreigners additional to those which apply to Swedish residents. Exploration work or exploitation must, however, be carried out through a registered Swedish branch office, unless a Swedish legal entity has been formed for this purpose.[167]

IV. Designation of Land

589. Pursuant to the Minerals Act (Chapter 9), a holder of an exploitation concession may request the Mining Inspector to carry through a proceeding for the designation of land (*markanvisning*). In such proceeding, the land area which will be used for exploitation is determined. Normally, a concession holder concludes an agreement with the land owner and holders of special rights concerned with regard to the use of land for the exploitation activities.

V. Revocation of Exploration or Exploitation Permits

590. Exploration permits and exploitation concessions may be revoked by the Local Mining Inspector if the holder does not fulfil its obligations pursuant to the Minerals Act or provisions in the permit or concession, or if there are exceptional

167. Cf. Act (1992:160) on Foreign Branch Offices, etc.

reasons (Chapter 6, section 3). In the latter case, the permit holder is entitled to receive compensation from the State for the loss incurred as a result of the revocation.

VI. Termination of Exploitation Concessions

591. When an exploitation concession is terminated, the concession holder forfeits its right to the land allocated to it under the Designation of Land. The concession holder also forfeits its right to the ore or mineral which has been worked or extracted but not brought to the surface or dealt with in similar way (Chapter 13, sections 1–2).

592. The concession holder is normally under a duty to remove buildings and other installations when the exploitation work has terminated. In connection with a termination of an exploitation concession, the Mining Inspector shall determine the duties of the holder in these respects. The concession holder is also under a duty to furnish a financial security for the proper fulfilment of these obligations (Chapter 13, sections 4–8).

VII. Compensation

593. Damage or encroachment caused by exploration work shall be compensated by the holder of relevant exploration permit (Chapter 7, section 1). The permit holder is under a duty to provide a financial security before commencing the work (Chapter 3, section 3). Unless the parties agree with regard to the financial security, the matter shall be determined by the regional County Administrative Board (Chapter 17, section 2).

594. The holder of an exploitation concession is under a duty to compensate damage or encroachment, which is a result of land being taken in use for exploitation activities. If an extraordinary disadvantage arises, the concession holder is under a duty to buy the land, if the land owner so requests. The concession holder is also, as the main rule, obliged to buy the land in question, if no Designation of Land (*see* paragraph 589 *supra*) has been carried out within ten years following the decision to grant the exploitation concession. The calculation of compensation will be made pursuant to the principles of the Expropriation Act (Chapter 7, sections 2–4).

595. Furthermore, the holder of exploitation concession, which has been granted after 1 May 2005, will be obliged to pay a special remuneration (a so-called mineral fee) to the property owners, whose properties are located within the concession area, as well as to the State. The mineral fee is 2 per mile of the value of the minerals won per calendar year within the concession area. The mineral fee shall be distributed between the property owner(s), who shall receive three-fourth of the total fee, and the State, who shall be entitled to one-fourth hereof (Chapter 7, section 7).

VIII. Permit Requirement for Exploitation under the Environmental Code

596. Under the Environmental Code, the exploitation of mineral deposits (including coal, oil, natural gas and uranium) is subject to a permit requirement under Chapter 9 of the Code (environmental hazardous activities), *see generally* paragraphs 486–491 *supra*. The permit requirement under the Environmental Code applies in addition to the requirement for an exploitation concession under the Minerals Act.

IX. Authorities and Supervision

597. The Geological Survey of Sweden *SGU* is the central authority under the Government, which deals with issues relating to the country's geological character and the management of its mineral resources. SGU provides general information on geological and related matters as well as advice in general terms on legal matters in connection with mineral questions, etc.

598. Compliance with the Minerals Act is supervised by the Mining Inspector (*Bergmästaren*). The Mining Inspector also handles applications for exploration permits or exploitation concessions (Chapter 15).

§3. The Continental Shelf Act

599. The Continental Shelf Act (*Lagen om kontinentalsockeln, SFS 1966:314*) is based on the Geneva Convention on the Continental Shelf of 29 April 1958. Under the Convention, each state exercises sovereign rights over the continental shelf outside its territorial water limits (section 1 and sections 3–5a).

600. Under the Continental Shelf Act, the continental shelf is defined as the seabed within public water areas (*see* paragraphs 155–163 *supra*) and the water areas outside Sweden's territorial limits, which limits are decided by the Government in accordance with the Convention. The Act provides that the State has the exclusive right to explore the continental shelf and to exploit its natural assets, albeit that such rights can be granted to third parties, subject to a permit from the Government (sections 1–2).

601. Further, the Act provides that the laying of *inter alia* submarine power cables and pipelines on the continental shelf outside the territorial water limits of Sweden is subject to a special permit requirement. Such a permit is assessed and granted by the Government (section 15 a).

§4. The Act on Sweden's Economic Zone

602. Additional provisions on the exploitation of natural resources and the erection of structures outside Sweden's territorial waters, in its economic zone, are set out in the Act on Sweden's Economic Zone (*Lag om Sveriges ekonomiska zon, SFS 1992:1140*).

603. According to the Act, a permit (by the Government) is required for certain operations in the Swedish economic zone, *viz.* the exploitation of minerals and other natural recourses, as well as the construction and use of artificial islands or other structures or facilities – e.g., offshore wind power farms (section 5).

§5. The Act on Certain Peat Deposits

604. The Act on Certain Peat Deposits (*Lagen om vissa torvfyndigheter, SFS 1985:620*) regulates the exploration for and exploitation of peat for energy purposes. The Act contains a combination of a claims and concession regime similar according to the same main principles as laid down in the Minerals Act (*see* paragraphs 571–598 *supra*).

605. Under the Act, a concession is required for the exploration for peat findings, as well as for the exploitation of such findings. Concessions for exploration as well as for exploitation are granted by the County Administrative Board, sections 2 and 5.

Chapter 4. Other Environmental Statutes

§1. The Environmental Protection Act

606. The Environmental Protection Act (*Miljöskyddslag, SFS 1969:387*) is one of the acts that have been repealed and amalgamated into the Environmental Code. The Environmental Protection Act is, however, still applicable with respect to applications for permits that were submitted to the authorities before 1 January 1999.

§2. The Planning and Building Act

607. The Planning and Building Act (*Plan- och bygglagen, SFS 2010:900*) regulates the planning of land and water. The Act shall ensure that the public interest is considered in the planning, and it includes provisions on building standards, different plans that may or should be adopted by the municipalities within certain geographic areas, implementation, building-, demolition- and land use permits, construction work, as well as supervision and inspection.

608. Each municipality is the primary planning authority. The municipality is obliged to adopt a comprehensive master plan (*översiktsplan*) for the entire area of the municipality. The comprehensive master plan is not legally binding but will serve as an informative basis for further decisions. For urban areas, the municipality normally adopts a detailed plan (*detaljplan*), which is legally binding and can create rights and obligations for those concerned by the plan. If a municipality wishes to adopt a detailed plan, it must consult with the affected property owners, tenants, etc. In addition, the proposed detailed plan must, as the general rule, be exhibited to the public during at least three weeks.

609. In the planning of land use, both private and public interests should be taken into account. Environmental aspects are often an essential part of the planning requirements. The implementation of the standards set out in the detailed plan is to be made by means of planning or in connection with building permits. A building permit under the Planning and Building Act is normally required for building and construction activities and for demolition activities.

610. The role of the municipalities as the primary planning authorities, may in practice work as a limitation for the Government (acting through its national and regional authorities) to enforce the national goals set of the prevailing energy policy contrary to the municipal interests.[168]

168. Cf. G. Michanek & C. Zetterberg, *Den svenska miljörätten* 451 (Iustus 2008).

§3. The Combustibles and Explosives Act

611. The Combustibles and Explosives Act (*Lagen om brandfarliga och explosiva varor, SFS 2010:1011*) applies to the handling and import of combustibles and explosives, *inter alia* natural gas, oil and other petroleum products. Its purpose is to prevent combustibles and explosives to cause unintended fires and explosions and to prevent and limit damage to life, health, environment and property through fire or explosion. The Act includes certain safety precautions for handling of combustibles and explosives.

612. The Government or the authority appointed by the Government – the Swedish Civil Contingencies Agency (*Myndigheten för samhällsskydd och beredskap*) – is authorized to specify the products that should be defined as combustibles and explosives, measures that should be taken in handling such products, and to prescribe certain safety, construction and location requirements on buildings and facilities in which combustibles and explosives are handled. Provisions to this end are contained in the Ordinance (2010:1075) on Combustibles and Explosives and the detailed regulations issued by the Swedish Civil Contingencies Agency.

613. Under the Combustibles and Explosives Act, a permit is required for: (i) anyone handling, transferring or importing explosives and (ii) anyone that professionally, or to a considerable extent, handles combustibles. A permit shall be limited in time and contain the requirements deemed necessary for handling of the combustibles and explosives. However, this permit requirement does not apply with respect to the handling of combustibles (e.g., oil) which are transported in pipelines for which a concession is granted pursuant to the Pipelines Act or the Natural Gas Act.[169]

614. The Swedish Civil Contingencies Agency, is *inter alia* entitled to inspect facilities, to receive any information deemed necessary for its supervision, to revoke a permit, to set a conditional fine and to order necessary injunctions and prohibitions.

615. Non-compliance with certain provisions of the Act is a criminal offence.

§4. The Transport of Dangerous Goods Act

616. The Transport of Dangerous Goods Act (*Lag om transport av farligt gods, SFS 2006:263*) contains requirements for transportation of dangerous goods in most types of vehicles (tank lorries, railway, aircraft and ships). Dangerous goods include *inter alia* explosives, gas, radioactive goods and combustibles. Transportation of dangerous goods should be made in such a manner that injury to people or animals, and damage to property and the environment can be prevented. Thus, vehicles used for transportation shall be constructed and equipped sufficiently to avoid such injury or damage. Non-compliance with certain provisions of the Act is a criminal offence.

§5. The Road Act

617. The Road Act (*Väglag, SFS 1971:948*) contains certain special provisions regarding *inter alia* the laying and maintenance of power cables or pipelines within

169. Act on Combustibles and Explosives, s. 16.

public road areas which as a main rule must be approved by the Swedish Transport Administration (*Trafikverket*).

§6. The Act Concerning Heritage Management

618. The Act concerning Cultural Heritage Management (*Lagen om kulturminnen m.m., SFS 1998:950*) contains provisions aimed at protecting ancient monuments, building monuments, etc.

Chapter 5. Climate Policies and Emissions Trading

§1. The Kyoto Protocol and EU and Swedish Climate Strategies

619. Climate change is a global issue, which is addressed by the international community. At the United Nations Conference on Environment and Development in Rio de Janeiro in 1992, 154 states signed the UN Framework Convention on Climate Change (the Climate Convention).

620. Pursuant to the Kyoto Protocol,[170] which was signed under the Climate Convention in 1997 and entered into force in 2005, thirty-seven industrialized countries (or 'Annex I-countries'), including the EU as such, undertook to reduce their emissions of climate-affecting gases 'GHG' by a total of at least 5% on average during the period 2008–2012. To date, more than 190 states have signed and ratified the protocol. The United States signed but did not ratify the Protocol. Canada withdrew from it in 2011. The Kyoto Protocol applies to six GHG – carbon dioxide (CO_2), methane (CH_4), nitrous oxide (laughing gas) (N_2O), hydro fluorocarbons (HFC), fluorocarbons (FC) and sulphur hexafluoride (SF_6).

621. At the Doha climate change talks in 2012, the parties to the Kyoto Protocol agreed to a second commitment period of emissions reductions from 1 January 2013 to 31 December 2020, by way of an amendment to the Protocol. The thirty-seven countries with binding targets in the second commitment period include all members of the EU. Collectively, these countries will reduce their emissions to a level 18% below their 1990 level between 2013 and 2020. The emissions targets specified in second commitment period will apply to about 15% of the world's greenhouse gas emissions. Negotiations were held in the framework of the yearly UNFCCC Climate Change Conferences on measures to be taken after the second commitment period ends in 2020. This resulted in 2015 to the adoption of the Paris Agreement, which is a separate instrument under the UNFCCC rather than an amendment of the Kyoto protocol.

622. In 2009, the EU climate and energy package was enacted. It is a set of binding legislation which aims to ensure that the EU meets its climate and energy targets for 2020. These targets, known as the '20-20-20' targets, set three key objectives for 2020: A 20% reduction in EU greenhouse gas emissions from 1990 levels; raising the share of EU energy consumption produced from renewable resources to 20%; and a 20% improvement in the EU's energy efficiency.[171] The EU Commissions has submitted reports analysing the effects of further emissions reduction to 30% by 2020, but no binding legislation to this end has yet been enacted.[172]

---

170. The Kyoto Protocol to the United Nations Framework Convention on Climate Change, adopted on 11 Dec. 1997.

171. *See* www.ec.europa.eu/clima/policies/package/index_en.htm.

172. For example, COM(2010) 265 final, Communication from the Commission, '*Analysis of options to move beyond 20% greenhouse gas emission reductions and assessing the risk of carbon leakage*'.

623. In 2009, the Swedish government decided on a new integrated energy and climate policy which was approved by Parliament in 2010.[173] According to the new climate policy, greenhouse gas emissions should by 2020 be 40% less than the level in 1990[174] and the country be carbon-neutral by 2050. Greenhouse gas emissions in Sweden, excluding emissions and removals from land use and forestry, decreased by 9% over the period 1990–2007 and are expected to continue to decline.[175]

§2. Flexible Mechanisms: In General

624. In order to reach the GHG emission reduction targets and attaining cost-effectiveness, the Kyoto Protocol allows for three 'flexible mechanisms', such as joint implementation, the Clean Development Mechanism (CDM) and emissions trading:

(1) *Joint Implementation*, i.e., one developed country carrying out projects in another and being credited with the resultant reduction of emissions.
(2) *Clean Development Mechanism*, i.e., a developed country carrying out a joint emissions reduction project with a developing country and being credited with the emission reductions.
(3) *Emissions trading* between developed countries, in such a way that a country which reduces emissions reduction in excess of its commitment can, but need not, sell emission rights to a country e.g., because such country may have difficulties in meeting its target.

625. The purpose of these mechanisms (all three) is to lower the cost of emission reduction, and to provide technology transfer from affluent developed countries to poorer developed countries (Joint Implementation) and to developing countries (Clean Development Mechanism).

§3. Emissions Trading: EU ETS

626. A number of Emissions Trading Schemes (ETS) have been, or are planned to be, implemented in many countries throughout the world. The EU Emissions Trading System (EU ETS) was the first large ETS in the world, and remains the biggest.[176] In the following, we will briefly summarize the main provisions of the EU ETS and its application in Sweden.

173. Prop. 2008/2009:162 and 163.
174. This target refers to the non-trading sector, i.e., the sectors not included in the EU Emissions Trading Scheme.
175. Ds 2009:63, p. 6.
176. For a general description, *see* e.g. *The Swedish Environmental Protection Agency*, www.naturvardsverket.se.

I. The Mechanism of Emissions Trading

627. As mentioned *supra*, trading in emissions allowances (emissions trading) is one of the flexible mechanisms included in Kyoto Protocol. This instrument is based on the setting of a cap on total emissions for installations in a particular region included in the scheme over, for example, one year. However, this does not involve imposing a cap on emissions from individual installations. Rather, a certain number of transferable emission allowances are allocated to each installation covered by the scheme. One emission allowance (EUA) entitles the holder to release one tonne of CO_2 equivalents during a defined period. In aggregate, these allowances correspond to the cap on total emissions in the region concerned. The installations included in the trading scheme must then, at a certain defined date, be able to show possession of trading allowances corresponding to the respective installations' actual emissions. The intent is that operators with high costs of reducing emissions should purchase emission allowances, which are offered on a market by operators whose costs of reducing emissions are low.[177]

II. Summary of EU Legislation

628. An EU scheme for trading in greenhouse gas (GHG) emission allowances was introduced by the EU as of 1 January 2005, on basis of the so-called Trading Directive 2003/87/EC.[178] The most important amendments to the Trading Directive include:

- Directive 2004/101/EC,[179] containing provisions on the linking the Kyoto project-based mechanisms to the Community scheme.
- Directive 2008/101/EC,[180] under which the aviation sector was included in the EU ETS (as of 2012).
- Directive 2009/29/EC,[181] containing new legislation for the third trading period (2013–2020), *see infra*.

177. A general description of the emissions trading mechanism is set out in SOU 2003:120, pp. 27 et seq.

178. Directive 2003/87/EC of the European Parliament and of the Council of 13 Oct. 2003 establishing a scheme for greenhouse gas emission-allowance trading within the Community and amending Council Directive 96/61/EC.

179. Directive 2004/101/EC of the European Parliament and of the Council of 27 Oct. 2004 amending Directive 2003/87/EC establishing a scheme for greenhouse gas emission allowance trading within the Community, in respect of the Kyoto Protocol's project mechanisms.

180. Directive 2008/101/EC of the European Parliament and of the Council of 19 Nov. 2008 amending Directive 2003/87/EC so as to include aviation activities in the scheme for greenhouse gas emission allowance trading within the Community.

181. Directive 2009/29/EC of the European Parliament and of the Council of 23 Apr. 2009 amending Directive 2003/87/EC so as to improve and extend the greenhouse gas emission allowance trading scheme of the Community.

629. The Trading Directive 2003/87/EC, (as amended) has been implemented in Swedish law mainly by way of the Act on Emissions Trading and the Ordinance on Emissions Trading, *see infra*.

630. In addition, a number of Commission regulations with relevance for the EU ETS apply directly as Swedish law, including:

- Regulation no. 389/2013), under which a harmonized union registry for EUAs has been established.Regulation no. 600/2012, containing rules on the verification of greenhouse gas emission reports and the accreditation of verifiers pursuant to the Trading Directive.
- Regulation no. 601/2012, regarding the monitoring and reporting of greenhouse gas emissions pursuant to the Trading Directive.
- Regulation no. 1123/2013, on determining international credit entitlements pursuant to the Trading Directive.

631. The EU ETS has been divided into different 'trading periods'. The first ETS trading period (a 'trial period') lasted three years, from 2005 to 2007. The second trading period ran from 2008 until 2012, matching the first commitment period of the Kyoto Protocol. The third trading period covers the period 2013–2020.

632. The most important changes, which have become effective at the commencement of the prevailing third trading period, are: (i) allocation based on a common EU cap with respect to the number of allowances; this cap will be annually reduced by 1.74% (the EU common cap is set by the European Commission, where the current cap means that GHG emissions for the operators within the system shall be reduced by 21% in 2020 compared to 2005 levels); (ii) the auctioning of a majority of EUAs instead of free allocation based on National Allocation Plans (NAP); (iii) harmonization of rules for the remaining allocations by way of product benchmarks; and (iv) the inclusion of additional GHG in the trading system, namely N_2O and perfluorocarbons. The price of EU ETS emission allowances has been lower than intended during the second trading period, with a large surplus of allowances, partly due to the weak economic development in the EU during 2008–2012. In 2012, the Commission announced that it would delay the auctioning of some allowances. It is also considering a structural reform of the trading system to create a balance in the market and raise the price of emission allowances and hence the cost of CO_2 emissions. Suggestions to this end were put forth in 2015 include a reform of the Trading Directive.[182]

III. Regulatory Framework for the Swedish ETS

633. The main regulatory framework implementing the Trading Directive has been established through the Act on Emissions Trading (*Lag om handel med utsläppsrätter, SFS 2004:1199*). Detailed provisions on the permit and allocation procedures, etc. are stipulated in the Ordinance (2004:1205) on Emissions Trading.

182. *See* : http://ec.europa.eu/clima/policies/ets/reform/index_en.htm.

634. In addition, the supervisory authorities on a national level, the Swedish Energy Agency and the Swedish Environmental Protection Agency, have issued regulations on registry matters (STEMFS 2012:1) and on procedures for permit application and allocation of emissions allowances (NFS 2012:9).

635. The regulatory framework established by the Act on Emissions Trading is summarized *infra*.

A. *CO_2 Permits and Allocation of Allowances*

636. Pursuant to the Act on Emissions Trading, operators, which fall within the EU ETS, are obliged to hold a permit for the emission of GHG, in order to emit such gases (Chapter 2, section 1). As to energy generation, the permit requirement covers *inter alia* combustion plants with an effect exceeding 20 MW (including facilities which are connected to a district heating network), mineral oil refineries and coke plants which generate GHG. The permit requirement under the Act also applies to certain other installations in the energy-intensive industry, namely production and processing of ferrous metals, minerals, and paper, paperboard and pulp.[183] As of 2013, a number of additional installations are covered by the permit requirement; notably *inter alia* CO_2 emissions from co-incineration plants and facilities For Carbon Capture and Storage (CCS), as well as CO_2 and PFC emissions from primary aluminium production.

637. An application for a CO_2 emissions permit shall be submitted to the County Administrative Board and contain the information set forth in the Act. (Chapter 2, section 4). To obtain a permit, the operator must be capable of monitoring and reporting emissions in a reliable manner (Chapter 2, section 5). Conditions regarding monitoring (metering and surveillance) and reporting shall always be attached to the permit (Chapter 2, section 7). Furthermore, the grant of a permit for CO_2 emissions requires that the necessary permits under the Environmental Code, or older environmental legislation, have been granted with respect to the installation in question (Chapter 2, section 5).[184]

638. Operators are obliged to report modifications in their activities that may require updating of the permit. In such a case, the County Administrative Board shall make a review of the permit and the permit conditions, and where required issues an updated permit. New operators are obliged to report that they have taken over the operation of installations, and a new permit will be granted, provided that the new operator is deemed capable of fulfilling its monitoring and reporting obligations (Chapter 2, sections 8–9).

639. Emissions of CO_2, which are subject to a permit requirement under the Act on Emissions Trading, must be covered by emissions allowances equal to the emissions. Each allowance will entitle the holder to emit 1 tonne of CO_2 (or 1 CO_2

183. In 2016, approximately 760 Swedish facilities were subject to the EU ETS.

184. In order not to prevent the mechanisms under the emissions trading scheme, conditions that aim to limit carbon dioxide emissions in permits granted under the Environmental Code (or older environmental legislation) must not be stipulated with respect to installations covered by the Emissions Trading Act. Existing permit conditions to that effect are automatically unenforceable; *see* Environmental Code, Ch. 16, s. 2, para. 4 and Ch. 24, s. 15. *See also* Ch. 26, s. 9, para. 5.

equivalent) during the relevant trading period (Chapter 3, section 5). A permit shall contain an obligation to surrender – at the latest on 30 April each year – emission allowances equal to the total emissions of the installation for the preceding calendar year. (Chapter 6, section 1).

640. For the two initial trading periods (2005–2012), all allowances were allocated free of charge to permit holders for each installation for which a CO_2 emissions permit had been granted. The allocation was based on historical and estimated emissions as decided in NAPs in each Member State. As mentioned *supra*, in the third trading period, a common EU cap for the number of emission allowances has been set, instead of twenty-seven national caps under NAPs. Moreover, a substantial share of the emission allowances (approximately 50%) has been allocated by auctioning.

641. Emission allowances that are not subject to auctioning will be freely allocated based on statutory production benchmarks instead of historical emissions. The Swedish provisions on allocation of emission allowances to existing installations and new entrants in the third trading period are mainly set forth in the Ordinance on Emissions Trading, *see* section 32b–32j, which in turn refer to a Commission Decision (2011/278/EU) on harmonized free allocation of emission allowances.[185]

B. *Trade in Emission Allowances*

642. An emission allowance represents an economic value and may be transferred and traded as soon as it has been issued. As mentioned *supra*, the operator's obligation to surrender emission allowances equal to the total emissions of the installation each calendar year will occur at the latest on 30 April in the following year (i.e., fourteen months after issuance).

643. It should be noted that, the obligation to *hold and surrender* allowances applies only for a specified group of operators in the EU, whereas the *sale and purchase* (*trade*) in allowances is intended to take place on a free market with, in principle, no geographical or other specific limitations.[186] Both physical and legal persons – not only the concerned operators – will be allowed to participate in the trade. Emission allowances are subject both to bilateral trade 'Over the Counter' (OTC) and to exchange trade, such as the Nord Pool power exchange.

C. *Legal Status of Emission Allowances*

644. Under Swedish law, emissions allowances – like electricity certificates[187] – are in general regarded as financial instruments[188] (*finansiella instrument*) under the

185. Commission Decision2011/278/EU of 27 Apr. 2011 determining transitional Union-wide rules for harmonized free allocation of emission allowances pursuant to Art. 10a of Directive 2003/87/EC of the European Parliament and of the Council.
186. The trade in allowances may also encompass countries outside the EU, provided that an agreement on mutual recognition of the EU trading scheme and the trading scheme of such third-party state has been reached, cf. Arts 12 and 25 of the Trading Directive.
187. *See* Part I, paras 212–222 *supra* .
188. Prop. 2004/05:18, pp. 38 et seq.

Securities Trading Act (*Lagen om handel med finansiella instrument, SFS 1991:980*).[189] In practice, the most important consequence of allowances being qualified as financial instruments is that trade – other than direct trade between the concerned parties – in allowances will require a licence from the Swedish Financial Supervisory Authority (*Finansinspektionen*) under the Securities Markets Act (*Lag om värdepappersmarknaden, SFS 2007:528*).[190]

D. Transfer of Emission Allowances and Registry Issues

645. The ETS requires that *inter alia* ownership, transfer and cancellation of allowances are registered. Provisions to this effect are set forth in the Act on Emissions Trading (Chapter 4), which refers to the detailed rules of Commission Regulation no. 389/2013, by which a standardized union registration system for emission allowances has been established. The Swedish Energy Agency has been designated as the national administrator of accounts in the union emission-allowance registry.

646. In line with the 'registration principle' applied under Swedish law with respect to other financial instruments, the registration of ownership of allowances in the union emission-allowance registry has important legal consequences. The Act on Emissions Trading (Chapter 4, section 14) stipulates that the person registered as the owner of emissions allowances in an account in the emissions allowance registry shall, with the restrictions as may be stated in the account, be regarded as entitled to control the financial instruments registered in the account. Thus, the registration of ownership in the union emission-allowance registry will create property law protection for the owner, i.e., protection vis-à-vis third parties.

647. Restrictions in the holder's right of disposal with respect to allowances, namely bankruptcy, distrait, attachment and sequestration shall, upon notification to the Swedish Energy Agency, be registered in the union emission-allowance registry (Chapter 4, section 11). It is not yet possible to register pledges over emission allowances under the Act on Emissions Trading.[191] Therefore, a pledge arrangement regarding emission allowances need to be arranged by other means, e.g., through a security assignment.[192]

E. Monitoring and Verification of Emissions

648. Under the Act on Emissions Trading (Chapter 5), the operators concerned are obliged to monitor and report on their own emissions of CO_2 (constituting the basis of the number of allowances to be surrendered) during each calendar year. Reporting must be made by means of written annual reports, which are to be examined by

189. However, the concept of 'financial instruments' and its application with respect to emission allowances involve complex questions that fall outside the scope of this monograph, *see* e.g. D. Hanström, ('Handel med elcertifikat och utsläppsrätter'), *FT* 2007 no. 3, p. 183 and Prop. 2011/12:143.
190. Prop. 2004/05:18, pp. 39–40.
191. Unlike electricity certificates, over which a pledge can be registered.
192. *See* D. Hanqvist, ('Handel med elcertifikat och utsläppsrätter'), *FT* 2007 no. 3, p. 183 (194).

accredited verifiers.[193] The report must be submitted to the supervisory authority not later than 31 March in the year following the calendar year to which the report applies.

F. *Annulment of Emission Allowances and Banking*

649. Under the Act on Emissions Trading, allowances are, valid only for the trading period for which it has been issued and shall be automatically null and void at the expiry at such trading period (Chapter 4, section 2 and Chapter 6, section 2).

G. *Penalties and Other Sanctions*

650. Pursuant to the Emissions Trading Act (Chapter 8), it is criminalized to pursue operations causing CO_2 emissions without the requisite permit under the Act if such operations are conducted intentionally or by negligence. The same applies *inter alia* to the submission of incorrect or misleading information in monitoring reports on CO_2 emissions. Sanctions for not surrendering allowances covering emissions during the relevant calendar year include the payment of excess emissions penalties by the amounts set forth in Article 16 of the Trading Directive.

H. *Supervision and Appeal*

651. The main regulatory tasks in the Swedish ETS are carried out by the following authorities under the auspices of the Government (cf. Act on Emissions Trading, Chapter 7).

652. The County Administrative Boards consider and grant greenhouse gas emissions permits and have the supervisory authority in this area.

653. The Swedish Environmental Protection Agency considers and grants emission allowances, and has the corresponding supervisory responsibility under the Act on Emission Allowances.

654. The Swedish Energy Agency is the national administrator of the union emission-allowance registry.

655. A decision by the County Administrative Board in permit matters can be appealed to the land and environmental court (Chapter 9, section 1).

656. A decision by the Swedish Environmental Protection Agency regarding allocation of allowances and certain supervision decisions can be appealed to an Administrative Court of First Instance (Chapter 9, sections 2–3).

193. A person accredited pursuant to the Act on Technical Verification (*Sw. Lagen om teknisk kontroll, SFS 1992:1119*).

IV. Geological Storage of Carbon Dioxide (CO_2)

657. Directive 2009/31/EC[194] (the 'CCS-Directive') contains provisions on geological storage of CO_2. CO_2 capture and geological storage (CCS) can be described as bridging technology that can contribute to mitigating climate change. It consists of the capture of CO_2 from industrial installations, its transport to a storage site and its injection into a suitable underground geological formation for the purposes of permanent storage. The CCS-Directive has been implemented in Swedish law mainly by virtue of provisions in the Act on Emissions Trading and the Environmental Code.[195]

658. Under the Act on Emissions Trading (Chapter 6, section 1 b), an operator within the EU ETS, which is otherwise liable to surrender emission allowances corresponding to its CO_2 emissions, can fulfil this obligation (in part or in full) by verified CO_2 separation, transport and injection to a CO_2 storage site.

659. In line with the CCS-Directive, third parties are entitled to access to storage facilities and transportation networks for CO_2, provided *inter alia* that sufficient capacity exist in the network and storage. Provisions to this end have been implemented in the Environmental Code concerning geological storage facilities (Chapter 28, sections 14–19) and in the Pipelines Act with respect to certain transportation networks; i.e., pipelines subject to a concession requirement under the said Act (section 8a–8d).

660. The installations and infrastructure required for transport and storage of CO_2 are subject to permit requirements under the following main provisions. CO_2 storage facilities require a permit by a land and environmental court under the Environmental Code (Chapter 9). However, the Government will always assess the permissibility of such operations, unless the storage is constructed for research purposes and concerns storage less than 100,000 cubic metre CO_2. (Chapter 17, section 1, item 5). The Government may issue general provisions on the delimitation of storage sites (Chapter 4, section 9). If a geological storage is located in the sea on the continental shelf, a permit under the Continental Shelf Act will also be required, *see* paragraphs 599 et seq. Moreover, transportation networks (pipelines) for CO_2 with a length exceeding 20 kilometre are as the main rule subject to a concession under Pipelines Act.

194. Directive 2009/31/EC of the European Parliament and of the Council of 23 Apr. 2009 on the geological storage of carbon dioxide and amending Council Directive 85/337/EEC, European Parliament and Council Directives 2000/60/EC, 2001/80/EC, 2004/35/EC, 2006/12/EC, 2008/1/EC and Regulation (EC) No. 1013/2006.

195. Prop. 2011/12:125.

Chapter 6. Land and Cadastral Legislation

§1. General Background

661. In order to construct and use energy facilities and installations, such as energy production plants, electricity power cables for transmission of electricity or pipelines for transmission of natural gas as well as district heating, on land owned by another party, the operator of such facilities or installations must – apart from the possibility of purchasing the land which is needed – either conclude one or several agreements with the concerned property owners on mutually voluntary basis, or apply for some kind compulsory measures (*tvångsupplåtelse*) to the relevant public authorities.

662. In the following, a brief overview is given of certain parts of Swedish land legislation which are of particular interest in the above context. As to the special questions relating to water rights, reference is made to paragraphs 155–163 *supra.*

§2. Right of User Agreements

663. Pursuant to the Land Code (*Jordabalk, SFS 1970:994*), which contains the fundamental provisions of Swedish land legislation, an agreement on the grant of right of user (*nyttjanderättsavtal*), other than site leasehold (*tomträtt*) is not binding for more than fifty years from the date on which the agreement was concluded. Within an area covered by a detailed development plan pursuant to the Planning and Building Act (*see* paragraphs 607–610 *supra*), the maximum duration is, however, limited to twenty-five years. Said time limitations do not apply to right of user granted by the State, where the duration of the agreement may be determined to an indefinite period of time (Land Code Chapter 7, section 5).

664. Special provisions apply to certain kinds of right of user agreements, such as ground lease (*arrende*) and rental tenure (*hyra*), *see* Land Code Chapters 8–12.

§3. Right to Electrical Power

665. Under the Land Code (Chapters 7 and 15), certain special rules apply to agreements by which a right to electrical power is granted.

666. A right to electrical power for lighting, motive power or other such purpose may be granted in a property unit to which an electrical power station belongs. The term 'electrical power station' refers to a generator, transformer, converter, accumulator or switching station.

667. The grant of a right to electrical power may be made for an indefinite period (Chapter 7, section 6).

§4. Easements

668. An easement (*servitut*) means a right in one property unit (the servient property unit) for the owner of another unit (the dominant property unit) to enjoy or otherwise use in a certain respect the servient property unit or building or other facility belonging to the same or to dispose of the servient unit with regard to its use in a particular respect. An easement may only refer to a purpose of enduring importance to the dominant property unit and must promote an appropriate land use (*see* Land Code Chapter 14). Common examples of easement rights are rights to use a road on, or take water from, another property unit.

669. Easements are granted either by way of an agreement between the concerned property owners in accordance with the provisions of the Land Code (Chapters 7 and 14), or through a cadastral procedure (*lantmäteriförrättning*) under special legislation (public easements). The consent of the owner of the servient property is not a prerequisite for the grant of a public easement.

670. Public easements can be granted pursuant to different acts, *inter alia* the Real Property Formation Act (*Fastighetsbildningslag, SFS 1970:988*), the Expropriation Act (*see* paragraphs 681–684 *infra*) and the Environmental Code (*see* paragraphs 155–163 *supra*, concerning water rights).

671. An easement formed by way of agreement under the Land Code, can, but must not, have a fixed duration in time (Chapter 7, section 6). Public easements formed through a cadastral procedure must not have a fixed duration (*see* Real Property Formation Act, Chapter 7, section 1).

672. Public easements cannot be formed with respect to a utility (line) which falls under the scope of the Utility Easements Act (*see* paragraphs 673–680 *infra*), *see* Real Property Formation Act, Chapter 7, section 2.

§5. The Utility Easements Act

673. Under the Utility Easements Act (*Ledningsrättslag, SFS 1973:1144*), a party wishing to use a space within a property unit for a line utility (*ledning*) can obtain a special statutory right to do so. This right is denoted a utility easement (*ledningsrätt*), *see* Utility Easements Act, section 1.

674. The Utility Easements Act applies to certain kinds of utilities, *inter alia* (cf. section 2, items 2 and 4):

- high-voltage power lines for which a concession is required under the Electricity Act; and
- pipelines through which oil, natural gas, heat, CO_2 or other products are transported, which cater to a public need and fulfil certain other general requirements.

675. In the sense of the Utility Easements Act, a utility includes devices necessary for the utility's purpose, such as transformers, pumping stations and other accessories (section 3).

676. The utility easement procedure is handled by the cadastral authority (*lantmäterimyndigheten*). A utility easement comprises, as determined by a cadastral procedure (*lantmäteriförrättning*), a power to take within a property unit those measures which are needed for the installation and use of the utility in question (sections 1 and 5).

677. A utility easement may, but must not, belong to a particular property unit or registered site leasehold (*tomträtt*). This means – unlike the ordinary easements described in paragraphs 668–672 *supra* – that it is not required that the holder of a utility easement owns a property unit to which his utility easement is connected.

678. Where a concession has been granted for a high-voltage power line, a natural gas pipeline or other types of pipelines subject to a concession requirement, the concession holder has, as a matter of principle, the right to be granted a utility easement in accordance with the concession decision (section 11).

679. A utility easement can be obtained also where the property owner does not concur to the location of the utility to his property. The property owner is, however, entitled to compensation for the damage and encroachment that the utility causes (section 13–13d).

680. A utility easement cannot be separated from its underlying utility. Therefore, the transfer of a utility for which a utility easement has been granted is valid only if the transfer includes the utility easement (section 35).

§6. The Expropriation Act

681. Under the Expropriation Act (*Expropriationslagen, SFS 1972:719*), a real property unit belonging to a party other than the State may be claimed through expropriation with ownership (*äganderätt*), right of user (*nyttjanderätt*) or easement (*servitut*), *see* Chapter 1, section 1.

682. Expropriation may take place *inter alia* for the purpose of a public need of electric power or other motive power, water, heat or suchlike utility. Expropriation could thus be made for the purpose *inter alia* of high-voltage power lines and pipelines for natural gas and district heating (Chapter 2, section 3).

683. As the main rule, expropriation entitles the property owner to full compensation at market values. In some instances, additional compensation of 25% of the market value or loss of market value is payable (Chapter 4).

684. Expropriation permits are normally decided by the Government (Chapter 3, section 1). Compensation issues in connection with expropriation cases are in the first instance handled by a land and environmental court (Chapter 5, section 1).

Part V. Interaction between Energy Law and Competition Law

Chapter 1. Introduction

685. The deregulation of the markets, previously monopolized by the State, in order to subject them to competition to the ultimate benefit of consumers, could be described as a general and continuing development trend in many countries, both within the EU and elsewhere in the industrialized world.

686. In general, a characteristic feature of these markets is the existence of a network (e.g., power lines, pipelines, railroads, telecommunication facilities, etc.), which, in terms of economics, constitute (in varying degrees) a natural monopoly. In order to create competition with respect to the 'product' which is connected to such networks (e.g., electricity, natural gas, railroad transports, TV-broadcasting, etc.), there must be mechanisms enabling TPA to the networks on reasonable and non-discriminatory terms. Moreover, in order to avoid cross-subsidizing and other competition distorting behaviour, it is often deemed necessary to separate the operation of the network from other commercial operations which are linked to the network in question (e.g., trade in the relevant 'product').

687. In the Swedish energy sector, the predominant network based markets are the electricity market, the natural gas market and the district heating market.

688. The legal framework and special features with respect to said three markets have been described in Part I, II and III, respectively. The following main points deserve to be reiterated in the competition law context.

689. The Swedish electricity and natural gas markets are fully deregulated. Trade in electricity takes place on a free market subject to competition. On the natural gas market, all customers are able to freely choose their gas supplier. The district heating market is not deregulated in the same manner as the electricity and natural gas markets, although strengthened TPA rights were introduced in 2014.

690. In the following chapters, we will provide a brief overview of the general competition law rules that apply also with respect to the energy markets.

691. We will also provide a brief description of the market structure and competition situation in the electricity sector, which is the most important of the energy markets within the scope of this presentation. As regards the market structure in the natural gas and district heating sectors, general reference is made to Parts II and III, *supra*.

Chapter 2. The Competition Act

§1. Scope of Application and Relation to Other Legislation

692. The current Swedish Competition Act (*Konkurrenslag, SFS 2008:579*) entered into force on 1 November 2008 and replaced the earlier Competition Act from 1993. The Competition Act aims at corresponding, as far as possible, to EU competition law. The Act is modelled *inter alia* on EU competition rules regarding anti-competitive agreements and practices (Article 101 TFEU) and abuse of a dominant position (Article 102 TFEU). It is emphasized in the preparatory works to the Competition Act that the Act should be interpreted with consideration taken to the practice of the Court of Justice of the EU and the European Commission. Thus, the development of Swedish competition law is intended to mirror the development on the EU level.

693. The provisions in the EU Regulations No. 1/2003 on the implementation of the rules on competition laid down in Articles 81 and 82 of the Treaty (currently Articles 101 and 102)[196] and No. 139/2004 on the control of concentrations between undertakings[197] are also of relevance for the application of the Competition Act (Chapter 1, section 3).

694. The Competition Act is applicable in all sectors of the economy, including the energy markets. It applies to all persons or entities involved in commercial activities.[198]

695. The EU competition legislation applies as Swedish law in parallel to the national rules on competition. Thus, in addition to the national competition rules contained in the Competition Act, Swedish courts, as well as the Competition Authority, have the power to apply e.g., Articles 101 and 102 TFEU. The application of the EU competition rules requires that trade between Member States is affected (cf. Regulation 1/2003/EC, Article 3).

696. The special legislation enacted in connection with deregulation of previously monopolized markets, such as the electricity market and the natural gas market, also largely aims at enforcing competition and preventing discriminatory behaviours by the market players, e.g., by way of providing for TPA to networks and unbundling of network operations from trading activities. The special legislation in such areas, *inter alia* the Electricity Act and the Natural Gas Act (*see generally* Parts I and II, *supra*) shall in those respects be regarded as a complement to Competition Act, and a cumulative application of the different legal frameworks is envisaged.[199]

196. Council Regulation (EC) No. 1/2003 of 16 Dec. 2002 on the implementation of the rules on competition laid down in Arts 81 and 82 of the Treaty.
197. Council Regulation (EC) No. 139/2004 of 20 Jan. 2004 on the control of concentrations between undertakings (the EC Merger Regulation).
198. Cf. Competition Act, Ch. 1, ss 1 and 5.
199. C. Wetter et al., *Konkurrensrätt – en handbok 4 e.* 89 et seq (Thomson Fakta 2009).

§2. Prohibition of Anti-competitive Cooperation

697. The provisions in Chapter 2, section 1 of the Competition Act, which mirrors Article 101 TFEU, prohibit agreements, which aim at restricting, limiting or distorting competition on the market to an appreciable extent or lead to such results. Such prohibited cooperation includes, but is not limited to, agreements on price cooperation and different kinds of market sharing agreements.

698. The term 'agreement' in Chapter 2, section 1 the Competition Act has a broad scope and includes, as in Article 101.1 EC, concerted practices and collusion between undertakings.

699. As mentioned above, for an agreement to be prohibited, it must affect competition to an *appreciable extent*. The market share and size of the parties involved are important factors with respect to this prerequisite. The Swedish Competition Authority has issued a non-binding general notice concerning agreements of minor importance where the term 'appreciable extent' has been defined in quantitative terms.[200] According to this notice, an agreement is not deemed as affecting competition to an appreciable extent, provided that the concerned undertakings have a combined market share of at the most 10% of the relevant market with respect to horizontal agreements and 15% for vertical agreements. Companies with an annual turnover of less than SEK 30 million may enter into agreements restraining competition, provided that their market share does not exceed 15%.

700. An agreement or terms of an agreement which infringe Chapter 2, section 1 of the Competition Act or Article 101 TFEU are null and void, and may result in a liability to pay damages to another undertaking or contractual party where the infringing party has caused the damage by intent or negligence (Chapter 3, section 25). In addition, administrative fines or penalties may be levied, *see* paragraphs 709–713 *infra*.

701. Exemptions from the prohibition stipulated in Chapter 2, section 1 of the Competition Act are laid down in Chapter 2, section 2 (individual agreements) and section 3 (block exemptions) of the Competition Act. Companies are obliged to assess themselves whether their agreements fall under said exemptions and are in conformity with the competition law rules. The block exemptions are defined in seven separate block exemptions acts, and applies *inter alia* on vertical agreements, agreements on research and development, transfer of technology and specialization agreements.

§3. Prohibition Against Abuse of a Dominant Position

702. Chapter 2, section 7 of the Competition Act, mirroring Article 102 EC, prohibits the abusive exploitation of a dominant position on the market by one or more undertakings. Examples of abuse include the setting of excessive prices or dumping of prices, the application of other discriminatory commercial conditions, or refusal to supply.

703. A dominant position (which as such is not prohibited) means, as a rule of thumb, that an undertaking has a market position which enables it to prevent effective competition by acting independently of its competitors and customers and ultimately

200. KKVFS 2009:1.

of consumers. In order to assess whether an undertaking has a dominant position both the relevant product market and the relevant geographic market has to be defined. In order to determine the product market, it is vital to assess whether products are substitutable. The determination of the geographic market concerns in particular questions on transport and transmission and the costs thereof. The assessment of a dominance is based on a number of factors (each of which does not necessarily need to be critical), such as the market share of the undertaking on the relevant market, barriers for entry on the market, and access to infrastructure and capital goods or intellectual property rights.

704. According to Chapter 3, section 25 of the Competition Act, the abuse of dominant position according to the Competition Act or Article 102 TFEU may result in a liability to pay damages to another undertaking or contractual party where the infringing party has caused the damage by intent or negligence. In addition, administrative fines or penalties may be levied (*see* paragraphs 709–713 *infra*).

§4. Merger Control

705. The Competition Act's merger control rules provide for mandatory notification where undertakings concerned by the concentration attain a combined annual turnover in Sweden of more than SEK 1 billion, and each of at least two of the undertakings concerned has a turnover in Sweden exceeding SEK 200 million (Chapter 4, section 6).

706. According to the merger control rules of the Act, a merger shall be prohibited if it creates or strengthens a dominant position on the market, which could significantly impede, or be liable to impede, the existence or development of effective competition on the Swedish market as a whole or in a substantial part thereof. However, a merger may be prohibited only if such a prohibition does not involve 'the setting aside of essential interests of security and national resources' (Chapter 4, section 1). This is unlikely to apply except in very special circumstances.

707. From the date of receipt of a complete notification of the merger, the Competition Authority has a period of twenty-five working days during which it may either make a decision that there are no grounds for action or that it will initiate a special investigation. After a decision to carry out a special investigation, the Competition Authority has an additional three-month period in which to take legal action before the District Court of Stockholm (as of 1 September 2016: the Patent and Market Court) against the concentration. The three-month period may be extended by the Court, provided that the notifying parties agree to it or there are special reasons for doing so. It is the Court who assesses the anti-competitiveness of the merger in question, as well as orders for divestiture and other sanctions. The Court must come to a decision within a period of six months. An appeal against the Stockholm District Court's decision can be made to the Market Court, which must pass a final judgment within three months from the last day of appeal (Competition Act, Chapter 4, sections 11–16). As of 1 September 2016, the relevant decisions by the Patent and Market Court are to be appealed to the Superior Patent and Market Court.

§5. Administrative Sanctions for Violations of the Competition Rules

708. In addition to the private law sanctions – nullity and/or damages – resulting from violations of the competition rules (*see supra*), the Competition Act also provides for several administrative remedies (Chapters 3 and 6).

709. The Competition Authority has the authority to order a company to cease any violation of Chapter 2, section 1 or 7 of the Competition Act or Article 101 or 102 TFEU, and to issue orders or injunctions relating to the compliance of other competition rules. Such orders or injunctions may be combined with administrative penalties (*vite*).

710. In relation breach of Chapter 2, section 1 or 7 of the Competition Act or Article 101 or 102 TFEU (prohibition of anti-competitive cooperation and abuse of dominant position respectively) of the Competition Act, the Competition Authority may petition to the District Court of Stockholm that a special administrative fine (*konkurrensskadeavgift*) be imposed. The administrative fine may not exceed 10% of the annual turnover of the company committing the violation. Decisions by the Stockholm District Court on administrative fines can be appealed to the Market Court (Chapter 3, sections 5–23). As of 1 September 2016, such decisions are made by the Patent and Market Court and appealed to the Superior Patent and Market Court.

711. For companies having conducted a breach of Chapter 2, section 1 or Article 101 TFEU, the Stockholm District Court (as of 1 September 2016: the Patent and Market Court) may impose a prohibition on trade activity (Chapter 3, section 24).

712. Further, under the Competition Act, the Competition Authority has extensive powers to order an undertaking to provide information (Chapter 5). Upon decision by the District Court of Stockholm (as of 1 September 2016: the Patent and Market Court), the Competition Authority also has the power to carry out investigations, including so-called dawn raids in order to collect evidence where a forbidden anti-competitive behaviour by a company is suspected.

§6. Institutional Framework

713. The Swedish Competition Authority is the national competition authority appointed by the Government, in accordance with Regulation no. 1/2003/EC, for dealing with competition questions and matters. The Competition Authority shall apply the competition rules *inter alia* in the energy sector. Energy matters are handled by the Authority's Department 3. Further, the Competition Authority may make proposals to rule changes and other measures to eliminate obstacles to effective competition, as well as develops and disseminates knowledge on competition issues. The European Commission cooperates closely with national competition authorities, and the Swedish Competition Authority narrowly follows the standards applied by the Commission.

714. Two courts – the District Court of Stockholm (*Stockholms tingsrätt*) and the Market Court (*Marknadsdomstolen*) – are designated to deal with competition matters on appeal of decisions from the Competition Authority. Most decisions (but not all) of the Competition Authority itself can be appealed to the Market Court (Chapter 7). As of 1 September 2016, the Market Court will be replaced by the Patent and

Market Court (*Patent – och marknadsdomstolen* – a unit within the District Court of Stockholm). The Patent and Market Court will handle all competition matters which have been previously handled by the District Court of Stockholm or the Market Court. As of the same date, appeals will be made to the Superior Patent and Market Court (*Patent- och marknadsöverdomstolen* – a unit within Svea Court of Appeal).

715. As mentioned *supra*, it should be noted that the general courts also apply Articles 101 and 102 TFEU in private law cases. Moreover, general courts also deal with matters concerning damages pursuant to Chapter 3, section 25 of the Competition Act.

716. Finally, the Swedish Energy Agency has the task to monitor prices and price development on electricity and network services on the electricity market. However, the Energy Agency does not possess any independent powers to take action against violations of the Competition Act.

Chapter 3. Market Structure and Competition on the Electricity Market

717. As mentioned *supra*, in Sweden, power generation, as well as wholesale of electricity, is characterized by few firms with large market shares. Moreover, the larger power companies jointly own the nuclear plants. The three largest producers produced approximately 85% of the total Swedish output in 2011, where state-owned Vattenfall (which also is the largest generator in the Nordic market) accounted for 41%, Fortum 20% and E.ON Sverige 18%.[201] In recent years, important structural changes have taken place: In 2015, Fortum sold of it Swedish electricity grid operation business (forming a new entity called Ellevio AB) to a consortium consisting of national and international investors (1. AP-Fonden, 3. AP-Fonden, Folksam and Borealis Infrastructure Management Inc). In 2016, E.ON Sverige spun off its nuclear, hydropower and CHP production to Sydkraft AB (a company in the Uniper Group).

718. The Swedish end-customer market for electricity, where approximately 120 trading companies operate, is less concentrated, even though the large power generating companies jointly own several of the trading companies.[202]

719. Since the deregulation of the electricity market in 1996, a consolidation has taken place in on the market, where mostly larger power generators have purchased smaller competitors. Even though, up-to-date, no individual merger have been prohibited by the Competition Authority, the increasing concentration in ownership has raised general concerns about the potential for the exercise of an undue market power by the larger players on the market.

720. The increasing integration of the Nordic electricity markets –*inter alia* through the trade on the Nordic electricity exchange (NordPool Spot) – works to reduce the risks for individual or collective exercise of market power on the Swedish and the Nordic markets.[203]

721. The retail market for electricity is fully open to competition, and there is no price regulation. Electricity customers are free to choose and change their electricity suppliers, and in order to increase competition as regards pricing and other terms, the Energy Markets Inspectorate runs the comparison website *Elpriskollen*.

722. There is a political will to create a common Nordic retail market for electricity so that consumers in the Nordic countries could choose their electricity supplier freely and across national borders. The implementation of a common Nordic end-customer market for electricity is intended to increase competition on the retail market.

723. In order to create a common Nordic market, the Nordic regulatory authorities cooperate in the organ NordREG. In 2011, NordREG published recommendations and strategies to achieve a future common Nordic market and a market model for this. In

201. Energy Markets Inspectorate, *The Swedish Electricity and Natural Gas Markets* 36 (2011).
202. *Ibid.*, p. 43.
203. Report from the Nordic competition authorities, No. 1/2003, *A Powerful Competition Policy* (Copenhagen, Oslo, Stockholm), 20 Jun. 2003, pp. 97 et seq.

2012, NordREG presented a road map towards a fully integrated common Nordic end user market.[204]

724. In order to obtain a more competitive market, it is considered necessary that all actors on the market have simultaneous access to information which may have an effect on the market. Disadvantages by lack of information may lead to distorted competition. Thus, since 2011, the Nord Pool Spot has introduced a so-called insight council composed of representatives of the regulatory authorities in the Nordic countries and the Nord Pool Spot management. The council shall *inter alia* provide the regulatory authorities better insight and information on the bidding on Nord Pool Spot.[205]

725. As from 1 November 2011, Sweden consists of four fixed bidding areas on the spot market. These areas are a result of the decision by the EU Commission in April 2010, to the effect that Sweden was required to change the way in which Sweden handles congestions in the Swedish electricity grid, since the until then applied measures to handle congestions was considered to be a restriction in export, and thus anti-competitive, *see* further paragraph 234 *supra*.

726. The Competition Authority has in previous reports and in other contexts observed the general risks of the co-ownership of electricity generation sources.[206] The cooperation among primarily the three largest market actors may lead to negative effects, such as anti-competitive exchange of information and diminished confidence in the functioning of the market. The Swedish Government has unsuccessfully attempted to negotiate co-ownership limitations for the nuclear reactors. The Energy Markets Inspectorate has however proposed ethical rules for the industry regarding exchange of information between the companies, which have been adopted by the owners of the nuclear power plants. The observance of these rules is supervised by the Energy Markets Inspectorate and independent observers, appointed by the Energy Markets Inspectorate, that are members of the companies' boards of auditors.[207]

---

204. NordREG, *Road map towards a common harmonised Nordic end-user market*, NordREG Report 3 – 2012.
205. Energy Markets Inspectorate, *The Swedish Electricity and Natural Gas Markets* 41 f. (2011).
206. Cf. i.e. Swedish Competition Authority report *Konkurrensförhållanden på elmarknaden*, 2007-05-07 and Åtgärder för bättre konkurrens, 2009.
207. Energy Markets Inspectorate, *The Swedish Electricity and Natural Gas Markets* 39 f. (2011).

Part VI. Concluding Remarks

727. As noted *supra* (*see* Chapter 5 of the introduction), in the Swedish legal system, energy law does not constitute a legal domain with distinct boundary lines vis-à-vis other legal domains. So far, energy law has not in general been treated as an 'independent' legal discipline by Sweden's legal scholars. From a systematic point of view, in Swedish law most, but not all, legal issues relating to energy are dealt with as a special branch of environmental law. However, many legal aspects of energy are dealt with by other legal disciplines – such as real property law, tax law and competition law.

728. Energy matters – apart from pure competition and tax law questions – are to a varying extent regulated by different sector specific statutes, e.g., regarding electricity (the Electricity Act), natural gas (the Natural Gas Act), nuclear power (the Nuclear Activities Act), transmission of heat (the District Heating Act) and oil (the Pipelines Act), mining (the Minerals Act and the Continental Shelf Act), and certain aspects of hydropower and dams (Act on Special Provisions on Water Operations). In general, the sector specific legislation is linked to the environmental considerations to be made pursuant to the Environmental Code (in force as of 1 January 1999), which has a wider scope of application than earlier environmental legislation. As described in Part IV *supra*, the interaction between the sector specific energy legislation and the Environmental Code is in some cases rather complex, and does not follow uniform principles of application.

729. Another important aspect of Swedish law in the energy sector is the steadily growing influence of EU law. The EU has adopted a large number of Directives in the energy area, e.g., regarding the deregulation of the electricity and the natural gas markets. The EU also plays an important role with respect to the development of environmental law. Amongst other things, the world's first large-scale ETS, with the purpose of reducing emissions of green house gas emissions, was launched on a European level as of 1 January 2005. This scheme, which has been gradually expanded to new facilities and sectors, now enters into its third trading period which will last until 2020. The European Commission advocates major reforms of the trading scheme in order for it to effectively work reduce greenhouse gas emissions.

730. As far as Swedish energy policy is concerned, in 2004 the IEA described the earlier Swedish policy as a mix of significant government involvement in certain sectors and the reliance on unusually lightly regulated market forces in other areas. The EIA noted that on the one hand, Swedish energy policy was characterized by high and complex energy taxation, a political desire to phase-out nuclear power plants before the end of their technical and economic life span, and a market structure where the State owns one of the country's largest energy company (Vattenfall AB). On the other hand, Sweden was one of the first countries in the world to deregulate its electricity market, being a pioneer in the field of liberalized electricity trading as a part of the common Nordic Power Exchange (NordPool), and the State generally exercises a very light-handed regulation of the operators on the market.[208] The current energy policy, launched in 2009, still carries many of the features noted by the EIA in 2004. However, the current policy relies less on government intervention, which is manifested *inter alia* by the abolishment of the old phase-out strategy for nuclear power as well as the prohibition to construct new nuclear power reactors. These features of the energy policy were also confirmed in the 2016 political energy agreement involving a large majority of the Swedish Parliament, although there are currently no plans to construct new nuclear power. However, regulation of the natural monopolies in the energy sector has gradually expanded and become stricter, although this is rather a consequence of a legal development in the EU than the domestic energy policy.

731. Irrespective of the political goals of different energy policies, several crucial questions exist in the Swedish energy sector. In spite of recent legal reforms, one of these questions is the uncertain prospects for the development of new Swedish nuclear power, both due to very high investment costs and the lack of political consensus among the dominating political parties, which may involve additional risks for investors. Such uncertainties also apply to large-scale development of hydropower, which is prevented mainly by natural conservation considerations, and to a possible large-scale expansion of the use of a natural gas network, which has limited political support.

732. Moreover, the relationship between the energy policy goals – such as '*energy conservation*' – and the legislation in force, in various areas, is also of interest. The lack of uniformity in the legislation dealing, directly or indirectly, with different energy law matters, gives rise to questions on whether the rules concerned, e.g., the legislation on the planning of land usage (zoning), promote or obstruct the achievement of the energy policy goals.[209] In our view, the rapid development of energy-related legislation during the last ten years, especially through EU law, has created a need for further harmonization and coordination among the various energy law rules and related legislation, such as environmental law, planning and building law and tax law. In sum, it remains to be seen how the Swedish legislator will respond to the many challenges that it encounters in connection with the generation and use of energy.

208. Cf. IEA 2004, pp. 7 et seq.
209. Questions of this kind have been investigated in G. Michanek, *Energirätt. En undersökning från mark- och miljörättslig utgångspunkt med särskild inriktning på frågor om energihushållning* (Iustus Förlag 1990).

Index

The numbers here refer to paragraph numbers.

Made in the USA
Monee, IL
18 October 2026

66037581R10098